THE
BEST
OF
TWO
WORLDS

Books by JOSEPH WOOD KRUTCH

A Selected List

THE MODERN TEMPER

SAMUEL JOHNSON

HENRY DAVID THOREAU

THE TWELVE SEASONS

THE DESERT YEAR

Editor of GREAT AMERICAN NATURE WRITING

THE
BEST
OF
TWO
WORLDS

By Joseph Wood Krutch

Decorations by

WALTER FERRO

WILLIAM SLOANE ASSOCIATES, *Publishers*

NEW YORK

Grateful acknowledgment is made
to the following periodicals
for permission to reprint material
which appeared originally in their pages:

The Southwest Review, for "Don't Expect Too Much of A Frog"
(published in the magazine under the title "The Frog:
A Respectful View")

The Pacific Spectator, for "Things That Go Bump"

The American Scholar, for "The Best of Two Worlds,"
"The Microscopic Eye," and "Making The Days Seem Long"

The Virginia Quarterly Review, for "Harmless Necessary Mouse"
(published in the magazine under the title
"Mice—A Dispassionate View")
and "Presiding Over A Vacuum"

Mademoiselle, for "The Colloid and the Crystal"
(published in the magazine under the title
"Frost Flower and Christmas Cactus,"
Copyright 1950 by Street & Smith Publications, Inc.)

Acknowledgment is made also to *House Beautiful* Magazine
for permission to reprint, in the
"Post-script" to this volume, several paragraphs
first published in another form
in its March and November 1951 issues.

To O. J. CAMPBELL

CONTENTS

THE
BEST
OF
TWO
WORLDS

CHAPTER I

A MODERN PRIVILEGE

If all my days were spent as the majority of them are, they might not give me as much pleasure as they do. Nearly two-thirds of my time is passed in the country, and that does not always seem enough. But it may be that I am more aware of country life than I should be if I lived it all the time.

Your pure countryman, born and reared, is often satisfied with his life, and often would choose no other. But he is also very often a man whose interests and satisfactions are very different from those of us who have been transplanted. It is said that Mr. Bryce, for whom Bryce Canyon was named, left concerning it only one recorded utterance: "A terrible place to lose a cow in."

Country schools now give courses in "nature study" to the farmers' children, and they often need them almost as much as those bred in cities. Your farmer frequently grows up in an ignorance (the maintenance of which it seems difficult to understand) of everything in nature not immediately relevant to his profession. More than once—and plainly rather out of politeness to me than because of any genuine curiosity—I have been summoned to wonder at some creature described as strange, horrendous, and undoubtedly extremely rare, only to have it turn out a prevalent insect or, perhaps, one of the commonest of the salamanders. And how sinister everything not a regular part of his daily life seems to be! Every milksnake is a copperhead, every spider is deadly, nearly every weed is poisonous. I should be willing to bet that the famous brave man who first ate an oyster came from inland and that it was not a farmer who exploded the legend of the noxious tomato.

One friend who read something I wrote about the pleasures of living with some awareness of other living things, rebuked me for assuming that city dwellers did not know that pleasure. He spoke of the geranium on the tenement window which is all the more admired because it seems so improbable. He spoke even of Wallace's spider, and he might, though he did not, have gone on to speak of that stuffed owl, which, according to Wordsworth in his most solemn mood, brought comfort to a young girl long in city pent.

How such things may be, I know too well to question them. Indeed, I am prepared to go much further in making concessions about the city. It is more than merely the sense of contrast which gives me and many like me some kind of awareness of the natural world not common in those who have always lived close to it. We are really a new breed. When we speak of "returning" to something, we are using a wrong word. If we move wholly, or for a part of our time, from the city into the country, we are not resuming a kind of life which was once the usual one. The whole economic foundation of that life rests upon a complex urban civilization. And what is more important, our kind of sensibility, or at least our awareness of it and our articulateness concerning it, are different from anything which ever existed, even in Arcadia.

"I walk," said Thoreau, "as one possessing the advantages of human culture, fresh from the society of men, but turned loose into the woods." His was the best of two worlds, and he knew it as well as I do. We have that smattering of science which makes nature more wonderful, and we have also been trained in sensibility by reading. It was Thoreau, also, who proclaimed that "decayed literature makes the richest soil," and the man who made that statement was not one who was advocating any mere primitivism. To say that few men would fall in love if they had never read any poetry is true in exactly the same degree, and to exactly the same extent, whether one is speaking of the love of woman or the love of nature. Without thought and without culture, one might take a kind of animal delight in either, but he could not experience much more.

Certainly I feel no need to apologize either to myself or to others when I bring with me into the country whatever I may have learned from men or from books. Neither do I see any inconsistency in introducing into country life whatever from a different world may seem to enrich it. I see no impropriety in returning from an inspection of my marsh or from a walk in the snow to listen to Mozart's G-minor quintet on the phonograph. To me, at least, it sounds better than it would in a concert hall, and even those much more absolute than I in their condemnation of the gadget are only biting off the nose to spite the face when they refuse to accept whatever advantages may accrue from it while still being compelled, willy-nilly, to pay the penalties entailed. What I bring from the country into the city is perhaps less obviously important, though I am not sure that it is not equally so. I once used something I had learned from a mouse—she was a wartime refugee from Cambridge, by the way—to demonstrate in a review the unreliability of a certain biographer. But this is hardly the place to talk about that.

I have met few men or women wholly country-bred and completely without experience of life in cities, with whom I felt entirely at home. About them there is nearly always something *farouche*, if not actually savage. At some time in the course of his experience, every

man should rub shoulders with his fellows, experience
the excitement of a metropolis' nervous activity; live
close to the great, the distinguished, the famous, and the
merely notorious—if for no other reason than because
only so can he learn properly to discount them, or at
least learn in what ways they are, and in what ways
they are not, to be taken at their own and the world's
valuation. Those who, for example, have never seen an
author are likely to take books with the wrong kind of
seriousness! Urbanity seems to be literally that: something impossible to acquire except in cities. But one
need not, and one should not, I think, spend a lifetime
in getting it, for in that respect, as in so many others,
the city pays a diminishing return. The years between
eighteen and thirty should be amply sufficient to polish
anyone capable of being polished. If he is not urbane by
then, something more drastic than mere residence in a
city would seem to be called for. And if I have never felt
entirely at home with anyone who had never had any
experience of cities, I can say much the same of those
who have never had any other kind.

What seems to me so terribly, perhaps fatally, wrong
with the present stage in the evolution of the human
spirit is not its tendency to go beyond a mere "life in
nature," but its tendency to break completely the connection which it cannot break without cutting off its
roots; without forgetting with desperate consequences
that the human arises out of the natural and must always remain to some extent conditioned by it.

Beauty and joy are natural things. They are older than man, and they have their source in the natural part of him. Art becomes sterile and the joy of life withers when they become unnatural. If modern urban life is becoming more comfortable, more orderly, more sanitary, and more socially conscious than it ever was before—but if at the same time it is also becoming less beautiful (as it seems to me) and less joyous (as it seems to nearly everyone)—then the deepest reason for that may be its increasing forgetfulness of nature. She is often none of the good things which the city is, but she is almost always, nevertheless, somehow beautiful and somehow joyous.

Joy is the one thing of which indisputably the healthy animal, and even the healthy plant, gives us an example. And we need them to remind us that beauty and joy can come of their own accord when we let them. The geranium on the tenement window and the orchid in the florist's shop, the poodle on the leash and the goldfish in the bowl, are better than nothing. In the consciousness of the city-dweller, they ought to play a part no less essential than that of the sleek chrome chair and the reproductions of Braque and Miro. For me, however, I found them not enough.

Here, on the other hand, I have, literally, God's plenty. I am glad that the neighbors are not too near, that my little lawn and my brief paved walk end soon. Everything reminds me that man is an incident in nature rather than, as one comes to suppose in the city, that the natural is, at most, an incident, surviving precariously in a man-made world. If I do on my own a little of that peeping and botanizing which Wordsworth scorned, I think that I profit less from what I learn *about* nature than I do from what I should prefer to call the example she sets me—the example, I mean, of confidence, of serenity, and, above all, of joy. In the city, perhaps especially in the city of today, one may pass whole weeks without meeting a single joyous person or seeing a single joyous thing. One may meet laughter there, and wit—sometimes, perhaps, a fragment of wisdom. These are all good things which I would not willingly do without. But joyousness, as distinguished from diversion and amusement and recreation, is so rare that a whole philosophy has been developed to make a virtue out of its absence.

The world, we are told, is a terrible place, and it is wicked not to be almost continuously aware of the fact. Diversion in limited quantities is permissible as a temporary relaxation, but moral indignation should be the staple of any human life, properly spent. Yet it seems to me that Joy and Love, increasingly fading from human experience, are the two most important things in the world, and that if one must be indignant about something, the fact that they are so rare is the thing most worthy of indignation.

The limitations of the animal mind and the animal sensibility are no doubt so great that we can hardly conceive them. But no behaviorist's theory that the bird's song is merely a "sex call" or, as the more recent and therefore more depressing theory has it, that it is the male announcement of his claim to a hunting territory, can conceal the fact that the sex call or the "keep-out" cry is joyously given. From such phenomena I should like to learn, and I think that to some extent I have learned—though not very completely or very well, I confess—the natural way of making the processes of living joyous rather than troubling.

My very cats set me an example, for though they have taken on many human traits—though they can, for example, be bored, and sometimes irritated—I think that they have made little or no progress in what some seem to think the most praiseworthy of human accomplishments: the ability, I mean, to worry. They can be very impatient for food but, unlike men, they never seem concerned over where the next meal after that is going to come from. That is one of the reasons why I always feel more serene after a conversation with a few friendly animals than I do after an evening with even the most brilliant of my human acquaintances.

Or consider again the case of the birds. The most convincing explanation which has ever been given of the fact that so many species migrate to the north in summer to raise their families is not that food is more abundant—actually it isn't—but quite simply that there are more hours of daylight; more working hours, that is, during which the appalling amount of food necessary to feed the young can be collected. Now the spring just past happens to have been an unusually early one. Before the end of May, I noticed that my robins, their beaks already to the grindstone, were digging worms out of my lawn from dawn to nightfall. The summer was no vacation time for them. But they seemed not in the slightest degree resentful; in fact, they seemed quite happy over the whole business. What we call the cares of a family appear to be, for them, the pleasures of it. I think it is no mere pretty sentimentality to say that nature has remained joyful and that man, who has so much enriched his capacity for variety and experience, has lost a great deal of that capacity for joy, without which all the other capacities seem such dubious boons.

To anyone merely country-bred, I should certainly not speak of nature's superiority over art, nor should I tell him, if he happened to long for concert halls or art exhibits, that the wood thrush is in certain ways as much worth listening to as Isabelle Baillie, and the song sparrow is habitually in much better voice than a certain still-popular coloratura whom I had better not name. That would be worse than fatuous; it would be, for him, positively untrue. Whether one is inclined to say: "Nature I love, and next to nature, art," or whether one reverses the order of precedence, may quite properly depend largely upon how many opportunities one has had to experience his love for the one or the other.

But what I would not say to the merely country-bred, I should not hesitate to say to the bigoted metropolitan. If he asked me whether I did not feel seriously the lack of those opportunities for artistic enjoyment which, by the way, only a very few of the very largest cities abundantly afford, I should ask him to take a look at the fresh new moon above the tree on some clear, crisp evening, or even merely to compare the drive home through country roads from some sortie into the village with a return by subway—or even by taxi, if he happened to be one of those whose economic status permits him to remain most of the time above ground.

"But you do not seem to realize," many will immediately object, "how exceptional your circumstances are. Even among the rich, there are few who can escape the burdens imposed by their riches sufficiently to lead your kind of life as much of the time as you do. And among those who, like you, have a living to make, still fewer can arrange to make it as you do. Even granting for the sake of argument that the kind of life you lead is a good one, how could we possibly arrange society so that the mass of men could lead it?" "That," they will conclude triumphantly, "is the problem which has to be faced."

Now I have some kind of an answer to these remarks, but first I should like to say that the word "problem" is one which I did not intend to use even once, partly because its monotonous reappearance is one of the striking signs of our general unhappiness. Every civilization has certain key words whose constant employment gives a clue to the dominant tone of that society, and our tendency to see everything in terms of "the problem" is one of the clues to ours. We have not only the problems of government and economics, which are, perhaps, problems in most societies; we have also the "problems" of culture, religion and even of recreation. Indeed, we have turned other, even less likely concerns into other "problems."

Consider, for example, the case of Love. It has been, in many times, many different things. It has been considered in some ages primarily as sin. In others, it has been considered as perhaps the greatest of the mystical experiences. In still others, it has been merely a game or a diversion. But in ours alone it has become simply "the problem of sex." And the curious fact is that certain "problems" are rendered, as this one is, unsolvable by virtue of the very fact that we allow them to present themselves to us in the form of problems.

But to return to such answers as I can give. One, perhaps seemingly hardhearted, might be, of course, simply the denial that anyone who finds himself fortunate is morally obliged to refuse to enjoy his good fortune because all are not equally fortunate. It might be argued that to refuse to accept happiness if everyone is not equally happy would not be a way of securing, even ultimately, happiness for everybody, but merely a way of making sure that misery becomes universal, since even the lucky will not permit themselves to enjoy their luck. Such perversity may seem a virtue to those who

take certain attitudes, but it is perhaps not impertinent
to point out that it has not always been so considered;
that indeed, to Catholic theology it once was, and for all
I know still is, a sin—the sin of Melancholy which has
been carefully defined as a stubborn refusal to be grateful for the good gifts of God.

But it is not really necessary to take this position,
which many would find objectionable. The plain fact is
that most people would not want my life. I am well
aware of the fact that the majority of my acquaintances
do not envy, but, rather, pity me. If I should take their
inability to live in the country as "the problem" which I
was obligated to solve, I should conduct a campaign to
decentralize cities and to set the whole of a bitterly
resentful population to catching trains with the com-
muters, whom the majority of them despise. Plainly,
this is a case where the most applicable rule is not the
Golden Rule, but that Brazen Rule proclaimed by Bernard Shaw: "Do not do unto others as you would that
they should do unto you; their tastes may be different."
And in my particular case I find that they usually are.
The "problem" is made to vanish by the simple realization that it really isn't a problem at all. I think I shall
not use the word again in the course of what I have
reason, in experience, to hope will be a happy year.

For that part of it which I am permitted to spend in
the country I have not even—and I do not need—a
plan. So far as the grand events are concerned they will
be planned for me. I am no chanticleer burdened with

the belief that I have to do something to make the sun rise. Neither am I a druid convinced that it would not turn northward again in March if I did not implore it to do so. All such events will be taken care of by the most reliable of functionaries and the show will go on. The trees will bud, the grass turn green, and the humming-bird return from Central America where I have never been but to which he repairs every autumn. The liberal theologians of the seventeenth century said that God caused all these things to happen in order that man should admire His prowess and His wisdom. The less liberal nineteenth century said, through the mouth of Ernest Renan, that He arranged the whole spectacle, including the human subplot, for His own amusement. Even if this second view is correct I have at least re-ceived a complimentary ticket entitling me to a good seat and I don't intend to miss the show.

As for the minor events, I shall just let them happen. I have no project to work on, no special subject to pon-der. But in past years projects have never failed to sug-gest themselves and subjects for pondering never failed to pop up. To the best of my ability I shall play the amateur biologist and philosopher as the occasion de-mands. If I see something, think something, or remem-ber something which strikes me as communicable and likely to be even one-tenth as interesting to others as it has been to me I shall write it down. But I shall not feel compelled to do even that.

To the puritan, opportunity without responsibility

is rather more than anyone has a right to. And perhaps it is. But what shall one do when one finds oneself so unfairly favored? At least I am not concealing the fact that I seem to myself to be in many ways singularly, if not quite uniquely, fortunate. And if I do write a book one of its hidden subjects will be just that.

Chapter 2

THINGS THAT GO BUMP
IN THE NIGHT

Many years ago when I was still a cockney by conviction as well as by habit, I went with two companions
—one male and one female—to spend a few weeks in
what seemed to us a lonely house. Outwardly, at least,
we were brave enough during the first twenty-four
hours, but as the second twilight began to fall, a certain
uneasiness could no longer be hidden. None of us was
quite comfortable, and none quite willing to admit that
he was not, until the time finally came when the fact
was patent. "What," each asked the other, "are you
afraid of?"

"People," said I, "thieves, murderers, escaped luna-
tics—call them what you will—but people; evilly dis-
posed and strong enough to kill or maim me." "Ghosts,"
said my female companion briskly. But our friend still
hesitated. "Well," he said at last, "if you must know, it's
—panthers. I was afraid of them as a child and I am
afraid of them now. They lie along the low limbs of
trees, and they will leap upon my back if I pass under
them."

Then, of course, we went to work upon one another,
always two against one. No murder and no theft by violence had occurred in that region within the memory of
man, though both were common occurrences in the part
of New York City where we all felt perfectly secure
and at home. Even the fearer of ghosts admitted that
she feared them only between sunset and sunrise; even
the predestined victim of panthers was ready enough to
grant that no bobcat, even, had been seen in that part of
Connecticut for generations. And so we retired to our
rooms, each deprived of his pet rationalization but not,
I am afraid, much comforted in the place where we
needed comfort. And when, just before dawn, a squirrel
scampered over the roof, each saw in his mind's eye
what he was prepared to see: the murderer with his
knife; the ghost risen from his grave; the panther ready
to spring.

The country is a great deal safer than the city.
Nearly everyone admits that abstract proposition and
statistics support it. But no one who grew up in a town

really believes it in those nerves where the fear of the lonely dark takes its rise. Reason can reach the rationalizations with which we seek to make fear respectable to ourselves, but it cannot reach fear itself.

What we should have done, as I now know well, was to get a cat, or what is much better, at least two. Nothing else will explain so convincingly almost any of the creaks and groans to which an old house is heir. Puss can tiptoe or stomp as the mood strikes him and he can send tin pots and china crashing on occasion. He is equally likely to be in the cellar or on the roof and he might cause almost any noise one is likely to hear. In actual fact he will, of course, not be responsible a third of the time but nearly always he might be, and what one needs is a possible, innocent explanation of what otherwise seems to have none. Two cats are better for the simple reason that one is likely to be sleeping on your feet when you need him most and it is highly desirable to have a spare to fall back upon.

Of course not even a cat will explain everything which needs explanation when one is in the dark alone. When I was spending my first night in a rather out-of-the-way and rather ramshackle hotel in one of the more ancient and sinister towns of Italy, I was awakened about two in the morning by the sound of heels tapping smartly down the stone pavement. They stopped just under my window and I got up to look out. A man was peering intently at the door. After a close inspection he put some sort of mark on it and went on down to the next, which, after a short scrutiny, he left unmarked. This was during the early days of fascism, and I had heard that afternoon the distant shouts of a mob. What could this mysterious proceeding mean? I thought of the Passover and of the Massacre of St. Bartholomew, but I could think of no other explanation. When I awoke the next morning—and I am rather proud of myself for having slept at all—I hastened to investigate the mysterious sign. It was a little sticker assuring the owner that the watchman employed by some security company had passed at 2:00 A.M. and found all well. The explanation was as simple as that of certain strange tappings which kept my friends and me awake during our first night in the cottage. They turned out to be the result of the slow dripping from an old-fashioned icebox onto a sheet of tin outside my bedroom window. But why did I not think of that? Simply because, I suppose, when one is alone in a strange place, one does not easily imagine innocent things.

The place where I now am and where I spent last night alone is far from strange. I have known it for more than fifteen years and know it better than I have ever known any other place on earth. It is here and here only that I ever really feel "at home." But I have been alone in this house only on rare occasions. I need to remind myself that I am no longer the cockney I was twenty-five years ago and that I do not really anticipate attack by lunatic, ghost, or crouching panther.

The solitude I know best is the *solitude à deux* and that is the kind I prefer. Unfortunately, however, one cannot always choose. For thirty-six hours I have spoken to no human being, and that is long enough to begin to get the taste of aloneness into one's mouth. This familiar place—this most familiar and beloved of all places—begins to seem strange, at least in the sense of seeming odd. With no one to distract my attention, I get to know it better than I have ever known it before, and that in itself is pleasant. But out of the greater intimacy grows an oddness. It is like repeating a word until one seems never to have heard it before or like staring in a mirror until one seems to see a stranger. "Who," one asks, "is staring so fixedly beyond the magic pane?" "Is this," one asks, "the chair I have so many times sat in?" "Am I falling into a dream or is this the only time I have ever been really awake?" Perhaps, I conclude, man is always a stranger to himself. Perhaps only the presence of others who seem to know him makes him able to take himself for granted. When there is no one present to help him pretend, he knows that all is strange and that the strangest of all is himself. Those who are never really happy except in groups or crowds must have more fear of themselves than those of us for whom one companion at a time is usually enough.

When I look out of the window I see that though the ground is covered with snow, the day is—or at least ought to be—bright and cheerful. But I look away from the white expanse, and when I turn on the radio, the

sounds which come out have a ghostly air I have never
been aware of before. Somehow I am not as sure as I
usually am that there is really someone at the other end.
Perhaps a transcription is being played and perhaps
the engineers all died a few moments ago, along with
all the rest of the human race except me. Astronomers
are fond of telling us that when one of the stars disap-
pears no one on earth is aware of the fact until thousands of years later. The mechanical arrangements of a
broadcasting station provide a similar, if shorter, time
lag. Someone was there not very long ago. But I cannot
really know that anyone is there now. Perhaps the
turntable still spins, but spins for me alone.

The two cats are a comfort. At least something besides me is still alive. But is it only a fancy on my part
that they sense the fact that they are now two to one
and that I have no one to back me up? Is it only a
fancy that they seem, when they express a desire for
something, to make it slightly less a request, slightly
more a command?

Even under normal conditions they sometimes give
me what I call "the silent treatment." This means that
when, for instance, they want their breakfast, and my
companion, instead of preparing it, is making coffee for
herself and for me, they sit motionless and silent but
with their great eyes fixed upon her in a relentless stare,
as though they were saying: "Don't try to forget that
we are here, don't pretend you don't see us; don't think
we do not know that you are ministering to yourself

rather than to us. We are patient, and well behaved, and forgiving, but we know well enough how much we have to put up with."

Is it a fancy, I ask again, that the stare is now slightly more authoritative? A few moments ago I got it, as I frequently do, in the form of a suggestion that the chair in which I am sitting is well known to be this particular cat's rightful possession, and that if I had any decency in me I would resign it to its real owner. But would not the matter have rested there had I not been alone and had this been one of the rare occasions when I persist in my usurpation? Would the cat have leaped suddenly behind my back, squeezed into the small place available, and indicated quite clearly that even I could see now that there was not room enough for both? Even in the existing circumstances I am not really afraid of my cats. I think that they like me and I think that if the situation were reversed, they would make a pet of me as I make pets of them. But the threat of *force majeure* is something of which they are always aware in the background of their lives, and probably in a world where cats were dominant, I should be aware of the same thing.

Once long ago when I was just in the process of learning to feel secure outside a city, I had much more strongly the sense that the animal kingdom might be about to take over. It was, as a matter of fact, on the very first occasion when I spent a night in the country absolutely alone, and I had just begun to be aware of what seemed to be the changed attitude of the three cats I then had. There was a clatter outside the kitchen door. When I went to investigate I found the garbage can upset and two beady, ratlike eyes peering at me from the head of an animal many times larger than the largest rat. It seemed to threaten rather than to show any sign of retreating and I did not know then that possums sometimes do not run away, less because they are bold than because they are dim-witted and cannot move very fast at best. I retreated, wondering whether that possum knew that I was alone, and had hardly seated myself again when there was a rustle from a closet in the next room. When I opened its door, there, erect on its haunches and staring at me with eyes even more threatening than those of the possum, was a little white-footed field mouse.

When angry, mice beat a furious tattoo with their tails, just as angry rabbits, having no tail to flap, drum fiercely with their hind legs. Mice, I had been taught to believe, were timorous creatures. What, except a knowledge that the signal for the revolution of the animals against man had been given, could have caused this one to face me boldly and to say, as he was so plainly saying: "Get out, get out, get out"? I closed the door hastily and I did not call the cats, less because of the humanitarianism which would ordinarily have restrained me than because I was sure it would do no good. By now, cats and mice would obviously be on the same side. The united front was an accomplished fact. So Alice felt repeatedly when the animals in Wonderland seemed vaguely to threaten her, and I suspect that one of the fascinations of the account of her adventures arises out of the presence, just below the consciousness of most of us, of the unrecognized fear that someday the furs, the feathers, the horny shells, and the cold scales may take over.

Children like to frighten themselves. Two together on a dark though familiar street at night will begin playfully to suggest, one to another, that something dangerous is following them, until, presently, both believe what neither had believed at the beginning. That, I suppose, is a form of aestheticism; the love of experience for its own sake. And it is not confined to children. Last night I did not want to be alone in a country house but neither did I want to miss the fact that I was. And I toyed with the dangerous experiment of trying to frighten myself. Was I ever at any moment really afraid? Not actually, I think, but I could almost imagine that I was. And at that point I prudently called off the experiment.

Late this afternoon I asked the cats—in the tone of voice regularly reserved for that question—if they wanted to go for a walk, and they immediately indicated that they did. The sun was low as we started along the wood-road, and the more adventurous of the two—he who had had a sportsman's, rather than a proletarian education—ran ahead to the small pond across whose frozen surface he loves to slither and slide after the bits of wood I skim over the surface for his amusement. Often his hind legs fly out from under him though he seldom actually falls. I usually tire of the game before he does, and I do not laugh because, though he has some kind of sense of fun, he objects, as all cats do, to being laughed at. This afternoon I am not sure that I *could* have laughed. It is not something one does easily alone. There would be no more of it in the world if there were only the cats and I.

The glaze on the ice looked just a little different because I knew that no one would be waiting for us when we got back. I deliberately led the way to a relatively unfamiliar spot in the woods where we could look off an elevation across the wintry valley. But I had less sense of a strangeness than in the house—because, perhaps, I had less expectation that it would seem familiar. Under the circumstances, I half expected to feel at least the faint, faraway presence of that panic which the ancients attributed, not unreasonably, to the unseen presence of the wildest and most inclusive of the gods. But Pan snubbed me and made himself known only to the cats, whose fur bristled savagely and in whose eyes a new gleam appeared. Perhaps, like Minerva, he comes only uninvited. And on the whole I am not sorry that I did not meet him there in the twilight woods.

In a few hours now—long before midnight—I shall get out the car, drive to the railroad station to meet an incoming train, and in a few minutes after it has arrived, I shall not be able to remember why the last thirty-six hours have seemed so strange. What it is that my companion and I are able to protect one another against, I do not know. Neither has more power than the other to exorcise ghosts, and I am afraid that neither would be more effective than the other in dealing with any human aggression. And since it is not really the revolt of the animals that I fear, there seems only one possibility left. Pan rarely shows himself to more than one person at a time; for I, at least, am convinced that the panic of mobs is inspired by another and much more unpleasant god.

CHAPTER 3

NO BREAKDOWNS
FOR THEM

In this climate spring is no more than a brief, busy in-
terlude between a static winter and a comparatively
static summer, both of which sometimes all but over-
stay their welcome though spring never does. The hurry
of an arctic spring is, I suppose, even more frantic, but it
is almost breathless even here.

Shortly after the peepers begin to sing comes the
night when, for the first time, I see small moths in the
beam from my headlights. Then I know that the four or
five month period during which the earth teems has be-

gun to succeed the longer one during which cold has all
but sterilized it. Within the next week I shall almost in-
fallibly see the surprising little blue Lycenae butterfly
fluttering about plants which have only begun to put
out their leaves. And I am always amazed that, for all
spring's frantic hurry, she so seldom makes any mistake in the schedule which provides for each thing to
come in the proper order of its coming.

It is true that the robin often arrives in time to be
caught in the last flurry of snow, but he is a hardy bird.
Often he has spent the winter not in the south but
merely a few miles nearer the coast where the winter is
not quite so severe, and it is obvious that the possibility of running into snow is included in his calculations.
The phoebe, on the other hand, has never, within my
experience, arrived until just after the flying insects
upon which she depends for her livelihood have come
out in reasonable numbers. The schedule is very tight
and very dependable though the calendar which it follows is that of the earth itself rather than that of the
stars. Keep a record of temperatures for a few weeks
and you will know almost to the day when a certain
flower will bloom or when first the hummingbird, back
from Central America, will be seen at the trumpet hon-
eysuckle which is among the first of his favorite blossoms to appear.

Spring as a whole may be late or early. Indeed it may
be very late or very early, and the first of its obvious
phenomena may come as much as a whole month sooner

one year than another. But the order in which the phenomena occur is very nearly inviolable. Moreover,
things dawdle somewhat when the cycle has begun
sooner than usual and they all but tumble over one another when it has been delayed, so that only the earliest
happenings vary much, even by the astronomical calendar. Though April and May are often late or early,
June, or at least mid-June, almost never is. Every plant
or animal has its business to accomplish during the favorable season and it cannot afford to remain far behind.

Before the middle of June at the latest one is likely
some evening to hear fluttering at the screen one of the
giant moths: either the pale-green Luna with its extravagant swallowtails or the gaudier Cecropia, in red,
yellow, and black. Most people who see them seem to
think that they are seeing them for the first time,
though how anyone who has not spent his life in the
heart of a city can have failed to see one or another now
and then—or how he can forget anything so astonish-
ing, once he has seen it—I cannot imagine.

No individual Cecropia or Luna lives in this adult
form for more than a few days. He was a huge caterpillar the summer before and a chrysalis in a cocoon
through the preceding winter. He cannot, as a matter of
fact, take any nourishment, and the huge wings are an
apparently extravagant investment made for the sole
purpose of quickly finding a mate. Perhaps this is the
best possible arrangement in the case of an insect which

is not, as insects go, very plentiful and cannot, like so many of them, expect to find a wife or a husband on the next twig but one. Personally, however, I am by no means convinced that Nature Always Knows Best—merely that she has usually hit upon an arrangement which will work, even though, often, quite inefficiently.

Neither the male nor the female of these giants looks as though it was intended for so short a life. The female, especially, appears plump and flourishing. But as soon as she lays her huge batch of eggs the plump body collapses, and there is nothing left except a pouch of skin and the wide, beautiful wings. She was, as a matter of fact, little more than a flying egg sac.

The first thought of anyone who does see Luna or Cecropia is likely to be that this creature must have wandered up from the tropics, that nothing so gorgeously colored and so suggestive of the general extravagance which the tropics can afford could possibly be a native in austere New England. But the vague belief that nature is uniformly temperate here, that she practices only a kind of puritan good taste in decoration, is of course a delusion. Few spiders are gaudier than the yellow and black Argiope, which spins a huge web with a zigzag "signature" in any open weed patch. And could any tropical bird devise a more striking costume than the flaming red and the deep black of the tanager? Though she did, of course, acquire her taste for such display in South America where she spends her winters.

But to return to the Cecropia moth. It is, as I have said, not so common as many other moths and butterflies are. One might have considerable difficulty if one set out to find one on a given night even in the proper season. Yet the male and the female do find one another during their very brief adult lives. This fact puzzled Henri Fabre when he caught a female of a similar species but could not, by searching carefully within a radius of two miles, find a male, and he tried an experiment which I have repeated. Like him I confined the female under a wire screen and left her there overnight. Sure enough, next morning, several huge males were fluttering their great wings around the screen, though from just how far away they had come it is impossible to say. The desire of the moth for the star is only a pretty fancy, but this is a fact.

Supposing that odor must be the clew, Fabre went on, as I did not, with the experiment. What sort of odor could reach out so far? Could it be muffled by other odors? He tried surrounding the female's cage with assorted stinks—the most powerful he could find. It made no difference. The males, who apparently could smell nothing except the one thing they needed to smell, detected from far away the odor which no human being can detect even when it has no competition. It seemed unbelievable. Could it be that it was not an odor after all? Was it, as the naïve like to say when all other explanations fail, "vibrations," or was it "psychic"? Fabre tried a different tack. He kept a female for some hours on a piece of blotting paper. Then, just at evening, he transferred her to a different cage. Next morning the suitors were clustered eagerly around the blotting paper, while the expectant bride, her lure drained away, waited, forlorn and unnoticed!

If Fabre had lived in present day America, he would probably have thought, as I did, of the advertisements which decorate our magazines. Obviously if this were not a simian world but a lepidopterous one, it would be useless to offer "deodorants." Nothing could possibly mask the emanations, pleasant or unpleasant, of the body. What is perhaps more important, neither could any scent sold in bottles at a fabulous price rival them. There would be no point in those love philters called perfumes whose dangerously compelling force is described in advertisements employing the most lyric and most erotic prose of our time. Would even a copy writer dare to maintain that the liquid spell he is offering for sale is capable of attracting a male from as much as a mile away? Would any dare describe the results of a scientific experiment, attested by a panel of psychologists and physicians, which demonstrated that when a piece of blotting paper bedewed with two drop of "Nuits Délirantes" was placed on a sidetable in a drawing room, all the males hovered around it while selected beauties, dressed by the most expensive coutouriers, huddled unnoticed in a corner like so many wallflowers drooping on their stems. Go ye sluggard Chanels and Houbigants, not to the ant but to the moth!

The regularity of nature, her more than Chinese devotion to "that which is customary" has its other aspects. The housefly buzzing against a screen, even the bird who has wandered through an open door and flown over against an opposite windowpane, cannot reconsider the situation. The impulse to push forward when one wants to go forward is almost irresistible. In the end the bird, whether by chance or as the result of some finally dawning rational impulse, may at last get turned in the opposite direction and escape by the door through which it came in. Often at least, the housefly will persist until it drops of exhaustion on the window sill.

This unawareness of alternatives when the customary course of action proves fruitless may have, nevertheless, its compensation. Fiendish experimenters in a laboratory have recently demonstrated that by a series of carefully arranged frustrations it is possible to make a rat neurotic—though just why anyone should want to humanize an animal to this extent may seem difficult to imagine. Even more recently it has been pointed out by a scientific commentator on these experiments that this animal neurosis can be produced only in a human laboratory since it seems that seldom or never can the requisite situations arise in nature.

Your bird, fluttering against the pane, is not thrown into a state of baffled indecision. He cannot be because he is not aware of possible alternatives to the impractical line of conduct he has taken up. Even when an animal is faced with two irreconcilable impulses, he is not mentally frustrated. The bird, for instance, which has an impulse to return to its nest but also an impulse to flee from a human intruder who is inconveniently in the neighborhood, does not go off and suffer a nervous breakdown. It simply obeys one impulse to approach, then obeys the other to fly away; and though it keeps on repeating these actions until the intruder moves away, it suffers no frustration because instead of following neither impulse—which is what men do—it simply obeys each alternately. Your bird, to put it in Freudian terms, seems to have a lot of Id, possibly a touch of Ego, but no Super-Ego at all. In some respects he seems both as well and as badly off as the victim of the now popular frontal lobotomy.

As a matter of fact, when, at this moment, I look up from my typewriter, I see a small wasp, of a sort I do not recognize, crawling with futile patience around and around the surface of a screen, despite the fact that directly opposite and only a few feet away there is an open door. If the scientific spirit predominated in me I should leave it to its devices, and note, possibly day after day, the progress of its fate. But I am not predominantly scientific by temperament. Already I am beginning to feel frustrated even though the insect does not. I shall pause, remove the screen, and let it fly away— partly for its sake, but more, I fear, for my own. It was,

I noted on closer inspection, not a wasp but an Ichneumon fly. It has departed, and I can proceed with a question which it has suggested.

Why has no human defender of the more formal cultures never used the example of the never-neurotic animal to suggest the most obvious advantage of those social systems in which tradition, custom, and fixed forms of expression or behavior play a much larger part than they do in ours? The responses established by tradition are, to be sure, often inappropriate to a specific, unusual situation. They may become stupidities; they may even sometimes result in injustices or cruelties. But they tend to abolish uncertainty and bafflement. When the custom has been followed in a society which believes in the customary there is little puzzlement and little sense of frustration. One knows that one has done "what one ought to do." The occasional fly dying on the window ledge is unimportant to a race which, goodness knows, seems to get on far too well for our comfort. Might it not be argued that in human society occasional miscarriages of justice and the ruination, perhaps, of scattered individuals would be a small price to pay for general mental health? Perhaps the strain of trying to be too continuously rational, of balancing too many factors, is more than the human animal can stand. At least I recommend the argument to those less concerned with the individual and more concerned with society in the abstract than it is easy for me to be.

The question of the extent to which even animals can vary their conduct to meet unusual situations is much disputed; even more the question whether the insects—of all highly organized living things the most closely bound to the most intricate system of customs and traditions—can depart from them at all. Major Hingston, a British army officer, who used his leisure in India to make the observations which are the basis of his classic *Problems of Instinct and Behavior*, thinks that to some extent they can. He tells, for example, the story of a colony of ants which routed one of its regular processions across a steel rail, where, periodically, a certain number of individuals were crushed by a passing train. After some time a tunnel was made under the rail and all passed safely across. Apparently the ants came to realize that the rail was dangerous. But even Major Hingston agrees that such incidents are rare.

One does not need to go to India to make such observations. I can look up at the screened window of my study, as I did a few minutes ago, or I can remember the behavior of the birds who come in winter to the elevated platform of my bird-feed. The chickadees soon find the food put out for them and so do the woodpeckers who are accustomed to finding their nourishment while clinging vertically to wood, as they must do here to get the suet I provide for them. But the juncos are ground-feeders. They are not accustomed to get food above the surface of the earth. Accordingly most of them gather in flocks on the snow at the base, getting what they can of the lean pickings provided by what the chickadees have dropped and paying no attention to the plentiful store a few feet above their heads. Occasionally, however, a few individuals will discover it and they mingle with the chickadees on the platform.

Did they discover by accident that the food was there, or were they unusually intelligent, unconventionally minded juncos? Are they breakers of tablets? And what do their conservative fellows think of them? Are they considered dangerous radicals or is their behavior criticized as merely vulgar, not in accord with the best traditions of junco society? Of one thing I am pretty certain. Even though some may be able to break custom because they are unconventional by nature. I strongly doubt that any animal has ever been capable of transvaluating a value. They believe in absolutes. They agree on what constitutes the summum bonum and not one has ever proposed "a new morality." None, therefore, ever asked whether life as we now know it is worth living, and none ever committed suicide. These are exclusively human privileges.

I doubt that any animal would envy us these privileges even if he could know that they are ours. And I doubt it because I have never observed, even in the animals with whom I have lived most intimately, any sign that they felt inferior in the presence of something which I could do and they could not. My cats ask me to open a door, even to get up in the middle of the night to let them in through a window when the fancy strikes them to come that way rather than through the cat-door in the cellar which is always available. But they do not wish that they could open the window for themselves any more than luxurious livers wish they could cook or tailor a suit. They would rather eat the dish and wear the clothes. Making either is a mechanical task, and certain kinds of helplessness are becoming to the aristocrat. Who would not be proud to say that he had never been compelled to know how to open a door? Wasn't it said in illustration of Victoria's queenliness that she was the only woman in England who never looked before sitting down to make sure that a chair was there?

I know that an experimenter who raised an ape-child with a human one reported that the ape seemed saddened when it realized that it would never become a man, but that hardly counts because apes are not really animals. They are merely imperfect human beings. Everyone knows, as Plato pointed out, what a "good" horse or a "good" lion is, though no one knows exactly what a "good" man would be. But the distinction breaks down in the case of the anthropoids. A "good" chimpanzee would not be a chimpanzee at all. He would be a man. And that is obviously what he is, most embarrassingly, trying to be.

Real animals, on the other hand, are different. I have known not only dogs and cats but also geese and mice as well as other even more improbable animals who

were in many respects "humanized." By this I mean
that they had accepted with pleasure the companion-
ship of human beings, that they took a good deal of interest in activities not a part of their natural existence,
obviously preferred life in the midst of a family, even
tolerated or loved animals of another species, liked to
be talked to and got a different expression around the
eyes. But they never gave any indication of feeling inferior. When something quite beyond their compre-
hension is going on, they get bored; they do not seem
to feel inferior. Indeed, dogs and especially cats seem,
under those circumstances, to pity us rather than
themselves. If I pick up a book one of my cats, instead
of wishing he could read, often leaps onto my lap, puts
himself between me and the page and seems to be saying that if I must look at something, he will give me
something really worth looking at.

Men have spent a great deal of time wishing they
were angels. Cats, dogs, and the rest never seem to
wish they were anything else. To some this is lack of
ambition. But should we, perhaps, call it contentment
instead? The two are often terribly difficult to tell
apart.

CHAPTER 4

THE HARMLESS
NECESSARY MOUSE

Mr. James Thurber once complained that in his household they seemed "to have cats the way other people have mice"; but with me it was once the other way around. We had mice the way other people have cats.

In the beginning it was the war and the refugee problem which was responsible. One of the laboratories in Cambridge University had maintained for a long time a family of noble rodents which, like many other noble families, was perfectly ordinary in every respect except the fact that the family tree was a matter of careful record. Students of heredity did not want the line

broken if Cambridge should be bombed out or meet
other wartime disasters.

Accordingly the heads of the family were shipped
over to a geneticist at Columbia University where they
proceeded immediately to the chief business of a
mouse's life—prompt, immoderate, and continuous re-
production. In a few weeks the descendants had become ancestors and two of the original refugees were
presented to me. They were no longer of any Importance to Science because a geneticist, though he sounds
very much like a genealogist, is really the opposite. The
one is interested only in ancestors and the other only in
descendants.

My two were white—albinos, that is—and were supposed both to be females—which indeed they were,
though I had momentarily what looked like good
reason for doubting the fact. I soon discovered that
both, though very tame and charming, were, perhaps
just because they represented a well-known family,
rather unenterprising. Settled on top of a card-table,
provided with sleeping quarters and several tunnels
constructed of Christmas cards, they were apparently
quite content and made no move to climb down.

After they had been settled there for some weeks, I
left them in charge of the maid while I went away for
a visit. A few days later a long-distance telephone call
informed me that one had given birth to a litter of nine.
Since I was at that time shamefully ignorant, I had to
go to an encyclopedia to confirm my guess that the

mother had been with me too long already to have been in an interesting condition when I received her. Obviously her companion must be the father. "This," I said to myself, "reveals a nice state of affairs. The Professor of Genetics at Columbia can't tell a male from a female and that is carrying delicacy too far, at least for a scientist." But my indignation was short-lived. Two days later came another long-distance call. The other mouse had just given birth to a numerous litter.

Now, parthenogenesis, or virgin birth, is common enough among certain insects, but it would be almost as surprising in a mouse as it would be in a human being. Even the proudest families which find themselves threatened with extinction cannot do it that way. Some proletarian, living unsuspected in my wainscoting, had obviously exhibited the enterprise which the aristocrats lacked. This humble Romeo had climbed the balcony instead of waiting for his Juliet to come down.

Now, I exclaimed jubilantly, I shall have an opportunity to check up on Mendel for myself. The babies, still pink and naked, gave no clue. But if they had really been fathered as I suspected, then when the fur appeared it would be in every case plain mouse-grey. Albinism is a recessive characteristic and therefore would not appear in any issue of this first cross, though, of course, if inbreeding continued, approximately one-fourth of the second generation would be white, the other three-fourths grey.

Before long it was evident that Mendel and I were

both right so far as this first generation was concerned, and, before very much longer, so far as the next was concerned also. Within a year I knew mice very well indeed, not only scientifically but personally. We were having mice the way other people have kittens. And very much like kittens they are too, except that one has them even more frequently and more abundantly than kittens can be supplied by the most assiduous mother-cat.

The unauthorized love-match between the aristocratic lady and the man of the people turned out fine. The succeeding generations inherited the tameness and gentleness of the mother with the enterprise of the father. Soon a sort of family village had to be founded —a large, screened cage two stories high with separate boxes for the families set up by the grandchildren, a community dining-hall, and a community playground, complete with a miniature version of the old-fashioned squirrel-wheel in which young and old delighted to ride. Mice are among the most playful of all creatures and they devised endless games in the wheel—sometimes a tug-of-war in which contending parties tried to turn it in opposite directions, sometimes a co-operative enterprise with one clinging to the wire while the other rode him round and round. When the apparatus was full, would-be riders often queued up to wait their turn.

Besides being extraordinarily playful, mice are also extraordinarily devoted parents. Fathers will curl up with the babies when the mother leaves them for a few minutes; other females will do the same if they happen to have no babies of their own at the moment, and in fact are not always able to resist the temptation to kidnap the young, whom they take to their own nest. When it seems for any reason desirable to move a family, the mouslings are carried by the skin of the neck exactly as a cat carries kittens, though I once saw a baby, grown too large to be transported that way, led firmly back into the nest by the ear when his mother disagreed with him in thinking that he was not yet old enough to be allowed out. Mice are also fanatically clean, washing themselves and their young with exactly the same gestures a cat uses.

The sign that a new family is about to be born is a sudden frenzy of activity on the part of the mother who begins frantically to tear paper into bits and to carry it, piece by piece, into the nest, where it is arranged into a ball with a small hole open in the side. Tame as my mice were, they wanted privacy at this moment and if I tried to peer in at the opening, the mother would seize a bit of paper and deftly close the hole in my face with all the decisiveness of a ticket-seller in a French railway station when, suiting the action to the word, he announces joyously: "Le guichet est fermé" and goes out to lunch.

In even the largest and happiest families one individ-ual is likely to stand out, and so it was here. In this case the "personality" was a certain female, plain mouse-grey but carrying, as I knew from her families, the recessive albinism inherited along with, perhaps, some of the tameness of an English, laboratory-bred mother. Her name, for reasons totally inadequate and not necessary to go into, was Sabrina—generally short-ened to Sabe.

Sabe was unusually charming—even for a mouse. What I can have looked like to her when she was on the floor and I standing over her, I cannot imagine, but she knew me, or at least knew a human being. She would come halfway across a room to join me, hoping that I would extend my hand on the floor so that she could crawl onto it and be carried about. Especially she liked to be taken to investigate strange places—a bookshelf for instance. When I brought her close, she would climb onto the books, disappear behind them for perhaps three minutes, then reappear in the space left by some missing volume and wait expectantly at the very edge of the shelf until I extended a palm which would transfer her to some other spot. This would go on until one of us tired—and it was usually I. Once when I forgot to put her back in the cage and she was outside all night, she came running from a corner when I came in next morning and waited at my feet to be taken up.

Her end, like the end of nearly all mice, was sad. I noticed a lump on her back which I described to the geneticist and asked for a diagnosis. "How old is she?" he asked. "About two years," I replied. "Ah, then it is senility," he said. "That is very old indeed for a mouse. Few ever reach that age. You had better practice euthanasia, for if you don't the tumor will turn cancerous and she will die soon." "Is that common?" I asked. "It is universal," he said. "All mice that reach that age die of cancer."

The situation seems to be simply this. Mice, being completely inoffensive creatures, can play only one rôle in the general economy of nature—that of supplying food to other creatures. They are eaten by almost every carnivorous animal not too large to find them less than a mouthful—by, to name a few, cats, skunks, weasels, snakes, owls, hawks, crows, and even foxes, who can sometimes be seen in an open field, pouncing like a cat. No mouse, therefore, is likely to live long, and so thirfty nature does not bother to endow them with a capacity for a long life which they would so seldom have any opportunity to use. To keep the species going, she gives them, not the longevity which would be useless, but the astounding and precocious fertility which is, from nature's standpoint, just as good. But I, not sharing nature's detachment, think it a pity that a creature which so usually meets a violent death should be so afraid of it. The terror of a cornered mouse is unmis-

takable, and its eyes far too vividly suggest those of
the hunted man which seem to say: "I knew this was
bound to come. But has it really come so soon?"

None of Sabe's children or grandchildren ever quite
took her place, but one of them, while still young, fool-
ish, and not quite housebroken, was the occasion of the
greatest furor ever created in my household by a mouse,
and was ultimately responsible for increasing prodi-
giously the respect in which I hold the feminine head
of that household.

I had left him, one morning, investigating my desk,
and had forgetfully gone away for an hour or two, only
to discover when I returned that he had disappeared,
obviously through a crack in the wainscoting. He was
a very promising mouse whom I did not want to
lose, and, besides, I was not sure that he was capable
of looking after himself. Presumably he would come
out after dark to look for food but I did not want to sit
up all night either. To my conventional mind, the obvious solution seemed to be a live-trap, but though
I was in New York at the time, the city did not seem
to yield one. There were, of course, mechanisms for
strangling victims. There were also traps for wood-
chucks and other large animals, which obviously would
not do for a baby mouse. The situation seemed hopeless
until my companion suggested, rather timidly, that she
saw no reason why I should assume that a trap was
necessary. What that tenderly brought-up mouse would

want was comfort. If I left him some food and a good bed, he would probably accept both.

It seemed almost too simple, but I prepared a small cardboard box about three inches square, lined with cotton and provided with a mouse-size entranceway. I put it on the floor and went to bed. Next morning I hurried not too hopefully into the room. There was no sign of the mouse—but just to make sure, I put my hand over the hole and lifted the box. There was still no stir and I almost threw it aside without taking off the cover. But I did take it off and there, curled up in the cotton, was the mouse, too comfortable and too snug even to open an eye when the box was lifted and the cover removed.

Now this incident, as I said then and have often repeated, revealed the workings of genius, which consists in the ability to see a solution which the ordinary mind —represented in this case by my own—would not see. The solution was bold and simple, thus exhibiting two characteristics of most genius-solutions. And it was possible only because the mind which conceived it refused to be led to the impasse created when the habitual statement of the problem is accepted. "Catch" suggests "trap" and a trap is something you can't get out of. But here a bold mind broke this link in a train of usual associations. It saw that the unique aspect of this situation was that the thing trapped would not want to get out. And from that unique aspect came the solution.

Sometimes my companion thinks that I lay too exclusive a stress on this particular demonstration of her genius. She thinks, though she does not put it this way, that she has been at least as brilliant on other occasions, and when I enlarge upon this one, she may ask if some other incident, which she recalls to my attention, did not do her as much credit. But I am always compelled to say "Not quite." And if she seems distressed, I insist that the reason is simply that so favorable an opportunity to exhibit genius has never again presented itself. As Samuel Johnson once said, in explaining why brilliant writers often seem quite unremarkable in ordinary society: "Unusual talents require unusual opportunities for their exercise."

A change in my living habits which made it necessary for me to be away from home for considerable periods put an end to my living on intimate terms with mice. But not until I had learned a great deal. I was a subscriber to two magazines, one edited in the interests of the laboratory-breeder and the other for hobbyists like myself. I had even some idea of founding a new one, but I never got further than the selection of a name. It was to be called, with a slight bow in the direction of another well-known publication, *Good Mousekeeping.*

I have read that even a hungry kitten will not kill a mouse unless it has been taught to do so, and from my own experience I learned the obverse of this fact—

namely, that mice are not "naturally" afraid of cats. When one of my cats approached the mouse-cage—and he was of course quite fascinated by it—the mice were not terrified but tremendously curious. Often the cat mounted to the top, sometimes curled up there to sleep; and the mice, instead of running to hide, were very anxious to get close to him. More than once when he put his face down to sniff, a mouse would climb up on a box, stand on his hind legs to bridge the remaining distance, and rub noses through the screen.

Here was something very much like the lion and the lamb lying down together. At least the lamb was willing and the lion somewhat uncertain at worst—only because, I assume, he had been conditioned by past experience to regard mice as food. Why then is not Utopia just around the corner? Why do the people so furiously rage? How beautiful are the feet of those who preach the ways of peace!

The answer, it seems to me, does not lie in "human nature" *per se* any more than it does in cat nature or mouse nature. It is the world we never made rather than the world we do make which insists that we live as we do in bloodshed and hate. We have in ourselves no natural impulse to do that, any more than a kitten has a natural impulse to kill a mouse. We too have to be taught. But the thing which teaches us is something from which we cannot but choose to learn—the ineluctable contingencies of that part of the natural world which is beyond the reach of change by mice or men. If we do not live as it insists, then it is difficult to see how, as a race, we can live at all.

Perhaps it is some consolation to know that the fault is older than we are, but it makes the hope of any completely fundamental reform extremely remote. Even if human nature can be changed, the evil does not have its ultimate roots in the psyche. They reach down into physiology and, indeed, into that whole pre-human, even pre-animal scheme, which does not ask the cat if it must "hate" mice but which leaves him only one alternative if he should refuse to eat them. No feet walk more persistently in the paths of peace than the feet of the mouse. And yet what does it profit him—in this world which is, presumably, the only one a mouse will ever know? Merely the rôle of He Who Gets Eaten rather than that of He Who Eats.

Throughout most of nature, at least, there is so seldom a tertium quid. And that makes one wonder whether, at best, ultimate goodness can be practiced by any except individuals willing to take for themselves the consequences of it. Perhaps it is best to lose the whole world in order to save one's own soul. But perhaps, also, if ultimate goodness really is required, there is no other way of doing it.

CHAPTER 5

DON'T EXPECT TOO MUCH
FROM A FROG

Whenever I feel that I would like to see a frog—and you would be surprised how often that is—I have only to open the door of my living room and take two or three steps to a small pool in the shade of a large spiraea.

Before the fox got my two pet ducks that wintry day a few years ago this pool was theirs. For a full decade they swam gravely about on its six-by-ten foot surface, blissfully happy and apparently unaware that water ever comes in larger pieces. They also chased one another with dizzy playfulness around and around its narrow circumference, stood on their heads to search for the worms they never found on its concrete bottom, and splashed madly at least once a day for the shower

61

baths they love. From those ducks in their time I got many lessons in gladness and much moral instruction: A little world, I learned, is as big as one thinks and makes it. To be a big duck in a small pond is not necessarily ignoble. One can have Lake Michigan in one's back yard if one wants to. Water is much the same everywhere. It is better to use what one has than to regret what one has not. Where ignorance is bliss . . . If we are unhappy it is less often because of something we lack than because we do not know how to use what we have. Ducks want but little here below.

When, after a long and happy life—one had become a mother for the first time at the age of twelve years—these ducks at last fed the fox, I decided to keep frogs. I refurbished the pool which had leaked and gone dry, and because I am, I fear, a man of too little faith even in nature, I planned vaguely to collect from some pond specimens which might be persuaded to settle down with me.

I should have known better. Two days after my pool had been filled the first frog had discovered it and taken up permanent residence. Within a week there was at least one individual of the four usual species of this region: the two spotted kinds, Palustris and Pipiens, which most people don't bother to tell apart; Clamitans, the robust fellow with the green neck and head; and Catesbiana, the huge basso profundo who alone has a right to the name "bullfrog." Sometimes these frogs now hide in the herbage or under a stone. Nearly always, however, at least one or two sit on the rough, slab-topped rim of the pool—motionless, unblinking, sublimely confident that sooner or later, but always quite safely in time, some insect will pass by to be snatched up with a lightning tongue. Its unerring, flashing speed is proof enough that the frogs are not unaware of the external world as they sit, seemingly absorbed in meditation, hour after hour. Yet for all that, they are as exempt as the lily from the curse of Adam. They do not work for a living. They do not hunt for food. They do not even sing for their supper. They merely wait for it to pass by and sing afterward.

As the summer rolls along I hope that I may learn something from them as I did from their feathered predecessors. But whatever they may have to teach me will not be as easy to translate into human terms as the lesson of the ducks. Because these last were warm-blooded they were much closer to me in situation and philosophy. Gladness and pain were for us recognizably the same things. They could set me a real example when they rejoiced so unmistakably in the little pool which had to serve them in lieu of a lake. But the frogs are antediluvian. Like me, they are, to be sure, alive, and their protoplasm is much like mine. But they seem strangely cold-blooded in a figurative as well as a literal sense. No doubt they feel the difference between well-being and its reverse; their satisfactions may be, for all I know, as deep or deeper than mine. But their monumental placidity is something which I can hardly hope to achieve.

That is one of the reasons why I like to have them about, why I am so acutely aware of the strangeness of having almost at my doorstep these creatures who can demonstrate what to be alive must have meant millions of years ago when the Amphibia were the most progressive, the most adventurous, one is almost tempted to say the most warm-blooded and passionate, of living creatures.

I need do no more than notice the grasshopper just fallen into the pool to realize that, comparatively speaking, the frogs are more like me than I had supposed. At least neither their anatomy nor their ways are as remote from mine as are those of the insects whose tastes and habits sometimes shocked even Henri Fabre with their monstrousness. So far as remoteness of soul is concerned there is at least as much difference between the grasshopper and the frog as between the frog and the duck; perhaps indeed more than between the duck and me. The frog got to be what he is by moving in the direction which was to end—for the time being at least—in me. Even though land insects were newcomers when the frogs were already a well established family they took long ago the direction which was to carry their descendants further and further away from the rest of us; further and further from the frog, the duck, and the man. When I realize that, I feel that

Catesbiana and I are not so different, as differences go in this world, as I had thought.

At least one thing which I already knew the frogs have by now taught several visitors who consented to inspect them. Part-time countrymen though all these visitors were, several saw for the first time that the frog, like the toad, is not "ugly and venomous," but "interesting looking." And this I know is halfway to the truth that they are beautiful in their own fashion and ask only that we enlarge our conception of beauty to include one more of nature's many kinds. They are as triumphantly *what* they are as man has ever succeeded in being, and no human imagination could devise a new creature so completely "right" according to the laws of his own structure and being. They are the perfect embodiment of frogginess both outwardly and inwardly, so that nearly every individual achieves, as very few human beings do, what the Greeks would have called his entelechy—the complete realization of the possibilities which he suggests. Frogs are not shadows of an ideal but the ideal itself. There is scarcely one who is not either a froggy Belvedere or a froggy de Milo. To realize this one need only go to frogs as so many critics have told us we should go to works of art, asking first "What is the intention" and then "How well has this intention been achieved?"

I do not know what human being was the first to say that reptiles are not "vile" and toads not "loathsome."

I do know that these clichés lingered even in the literature of natural history almost down to our own time
and that perhaps most people still pick their way
foppishly about the world, rather proud of the distaste
aroused by almost everything which shares the world
with them and apparently convinced that nearly everything except themselves was a mistake on the part of
the Creator. Even Linnaeus expressed a distaste for
the Amphibia and the reptiles. Even Gilbert White,
who certainly knew better and felt better, absent-
mindedly falls into the literary convention of his day
and once refers to the ancient tortoise in his garden as
a "vile reptile." Most moderns are still far from catching up with Sir Thomas Browne who, three hundred
years ago, wrote into his *Religio Medici* something for
which I am very grateful: "I cannot tell by what logic
we call a toad, a bear or an elephant ugly; they being
created in those outward shapes and figures which best
express the actions of their inward forms. . . . To
speak yet more narrowly, there was never anything
ugly or misshapen, but Chaos. . . . All things are artificial; for Nature is the Art of God."

One of my lady visitors after looking for a while at
Catesbiana expressed the opinion that he was "cute,"
and I restrained myself because I recognized that she
meant well, that this was even, for her, the first faint
beginning of wisdom. I did not ask as I was about to
ask if the prehistoric saurians were "cute," if the
stretches of geologic time are "nice," and if the forests

of the carboniferous age are "sweet." As my frog gazed at both of us with eyes which had seen the first mammalian dawn, lived through thousands of millennia before the first lowly primate appeared and so saw more of the world than all mankind put together, I asked him to forgive the impertinence of this latecomer. The Orientals say that God made the cat in order that man might have the pleasure of petting a tiger. By that logic He must have made frogs so that we can commune with prehistory.

During the two centuries just past more has been written about the attitude of man toward the animals than in the two millennia before. Very little has been said even yet about their attitude toward us, and I sometimes wonder if that is not a coming topic just as its converse was beginning to be when Alexander Pope wrote his *Essay on Man*—which is, as a matter of fact, almost as much about man's fellow creatures as it is about man himself. At least until dogs and cats begin to write books there is bound to be a rather large element of speculation in any treatment of the subject, but we can imagine what some of the domestic animals might say, as Miss Sylvia Townsend Warner did when she made one disillusioned canine say to another: "The more I see of dogs the better I like people." That, I am afraid, is a bit anthropomorphic and so perhaps are the implications of my own frequent wish that I could hear the comments of, say, some wise, tolerant

collie on the conclusions concerning human nature to
be drawn from the juxtaposition of the statement that
"the dog is man's best friend" with the familiar ex-
clamation, "I wouldn't treat a dog that way."

It is not, however, in the spirit of either frivolity
or cynicism that I wonder what my frogs think of me.
They think something because they show some awareness of my existence and the nature of that awareness,
like the nature of the other relations between us, shows
again how much more remote they are than the ducks,
how much less remote than certain other creatures who
are, nevertheless, in some sense alive. It is hard to believe that the insects are aware that we exist at all
except as an impersonal force. In some part that may
be because, with one exception, they cannot turn their
heads over their shoulders to look at us. The exception
is the praying mantis and when he cocks his improbable head over his improbable shoulder, I have to remind
myself that he is one of the most primitive insects and
not, as this gesture might suggest, the most like one of
us. But I doubt that he, or a grasshopper, or even a bee,
takes me in as, in some realer sense, the frog quite
obviously does when he considers whether or not he
had better leap into the water at my approach and comes
to do so less and less readily as he gets to know me better. The difference between his awareness and that of
a cat or dog who can understand even some of our words
is immense, but perhaps no more so than the difference

between that of the frog and the apparently utter obliviousness of the insect who is shut off not merely because
he is less intelligent but also because such intelligence
as he has is so utterly different from ours. His standards
of value, if I may put it that way, are too irreconcilable
with mine, with cat's and with the frog's.

On a terrarium by my window is a huge ten-inch
salamander from Florida with whom I have had some
relation for eight or nine years. At least when he is
hungry he looks up if I happen to pass by and he will
waddle toward me if I offer a worm. Already my bullfrog will take beef from the end of a string when I
offer it, but he has given no sign that he connects me
with the bounty, and if he comes at last to do so, I
shall still not know whether it is more than a quasi-
mechanical association of a sequence of events. My old
housekeeper repeatedly assures me that the salamander
"knows her," and though I think that this is probably
a pretty large overinterpretation, I am not convinced
that the animal mind is as nearly a mere set of reflexes
as the behaviorists confidently assert.

I admit that in eight or nine years this salamander
and I have got into no very intimate, two-sided relationship, and this makes me wonder how much the
budding acquaintance between the frog and me will
come to. On his side, I imagine, it will not come to
very much; I will not mean much in his consciousness.
He is nearer to me than a grasshopper would be but

nearer only as the sun is nearer than Betelgeuse or Betelgeuse is nearer than the closest of the extra-galactic nebulae. The distance is still vast as we measure things. We can look at one another as the insect and I probably cannot, but we look across a gap as wide as that which separates the frog's origin in impossibly remote time from mine only a few thousand years ago. Perhaps some physicist who likes to think of time in terms of arrows which may point in one direction while other time-arrows point in the opposite, would say that the gap across which we look actually is a temporal one. I am looking back at him and he is look-ing forward toward me—across the interval which sep-arates the ancient time when he was the latest model from this present time when I am.

Perhaps I am already beginning to be an unimpor-tant part of his dim consciousness. But whatever intercourse may ultimately develop between us will be marked by considerable reserve on his part, and he will never want to climb into my lap as a certain goose used to do. A calm sort of mutual respect is the most I look forward to. Of one thing, however, I am sure from experience: whatever relationship we do achieve will be on the basis of reciprocal tolerance and good manners. The lower animals seldom bicker and at most usually suggest only that we should leave them alone. They may fight for self-protection if one insists, but they would prefer only to agree to differ. When my frog gets enough of my company he will show me a fine pair of hind legs, but he will hurl no insults and make no cutting remarks. He will say only, "I should prefer to be alone."

Perhaps this is partly because he can make a cleaner getaway than people can when someone bores them, but I have noticed also and in general that only the higher animals can be bad tempered. I have seen a seal deliberately squirt a stream of water into a spectator's face—in fact the New York Aquarium had, many years ago, a notorious member of that species who did this regularly to the great delight of those waiting spectators who were in the know. But that was only rough humor and I have never been deliberately insulted by any creature lower than a chimpanzee. That was when I set one such an example of bad manners by deliberately trying to stare him down as he looked from behind his bars. Presently, he turned his back to me with great deliberation, lowered his head until he was peering out from between his buttocks, and then pursed his lips to give me what is commonly known as a Bronx Cheer, though the present use of it seemed to suggest that it had been invented long before the borough was founded. I have never seen any other sub-human primate do anything which seemed so completely human, and I never at any moment in my life had a more lively conviction that we and the anthropoids really do come of a common stock.

My intercourse with the frogs will never be marked
by any incidents like that. Indeed it will probably seldom provide what could be called an incident at all.
But that is the price one must pay for escaping also
the possibility of anything approaching a disturbing
clash. His sang-froid is what the words mean literally:
cold blood. My blood is too warm not to want,
often, a more lively if more dangerous intercourse—
with ducks, with cats, and even with creatures as ex-
asperating as the members of my own species frequently are.

Much the same sort of thing I am compelled to admit
in connection with the frog's vocal comments. The four
species gathered around my pool—which of course they
legitimately think of as theirs—are respectively so-
prano, tenor, contralto, and bass. But what they croak
at their various pitches is the same thing, even though
it sounds weightiest when Catesbiana gives it utterance. The whole philosophy of frogs, all the wisdom
they have accumulated in millions of years of experience, is expressed in that *urrrr-unk* uttered with an air
which seems to suggest that the speaker feels it to be
completely adequate. The comment does not seem very
passionate or very aspiring, but it is contented and not
cynical. Frogs have considered life and found it, if not
exactly ecstatic, at least quite pleasant and satisfac-
tory. Buddha is said to have made a comment much
like theirs after all those years of contemplating his

navel, and though I do not wholly understand it I think I catch the drift.

It is not, I realize, quite enough for me whether it comes from the pond-side or from the Mysterious East. I cannot live by it all the time. Not infrequently I find myself responding instead to the more passionate observations of Shakespeare or Mozart. But in that eclecticism which serves me as a philosophy of life it has its place. It is basic and a last resort. I like to hear it preached from time to time and to think that it is something one might at least fall back upon.

CHAPTER 6

HE MADE SO MANY
OF THEM

The eight-year-old son of a widowed friend is becoming quite an entomologist. He is, however, considerably impeded in his efforts to make a collection by the reluctance to kill, even for scientific purposes, any of the creatures he wants to study. Not long ago when he had discovered on the garden walk a beetle of some unfamiliar sort he was heard to say, half to himself and half to his mother, "Gee, I wish that beetle would drop dead of heart failure."

Now from the standpoint of a child psychologist the real nub of this story lies in the fact that the boy's

74

beloved father had died only a few weeks before by
the hand of the very assassin he was invoking. By what
childish logic was it possible to reconcile seeming cal-
lousness with his perhaps preposterous sensibility? Or
should we, instead of asking that question, merely marvel at the naïveté which permitted him to attempt no
concealment of an inconsistency which an adult would
merely have hidden—even from himself?

One thing is certain. Though many students of the
birds and beasts never succeed in hardening themselves
to the point where they can kill without remorse, I
have never heard of an adult entomologist who felt
any scruple about depriving an insect of life, and I
confess that even I can work up little indignation over
the fact. Individual insects seem to have no individ-
uality in the sense that a bird, a mammal, or even an
amphibian does; each seems merely the duplicate of
the other members of the species. Not one seems to
possess any uniqueness which would make his extinction a loss, and so, though one might well hesitate to
extinguish a *kind*, one does not feel that anything has
ceased to be when one individual of that kind lies on
his back, the spark which nevertheless did animate him,
departed. We may admit but we cannot feel that this
spark was part of the same divine fire which keeps us
functioning and mysteriously aware of ourselves.

Of all living things the life in an insect seems the
least like the life we know anything about and the bug
seems less a fellow creature than even the paramecium

beneath the microscope for the very reason that, though
the insect's organization is infinitely more complex than
that of the protozoan, it is so radically unlike ours that
he seems more remote than a creature whose differences from us are more completely negative. The possibility of something like us still really is a possibility
in the paramecium. He has not yet chosen, irrevocably,
in which direction he will develop. But the insect has.
He has chosen to have his skeleton on the outside instead of the inside; chosen to breathe through open
tubes ramifying through his body instead of by lungs
which supply red corpuscles with the oxygen which
they will transport; chosen, therefore, to have white
blood which is not circulated through veins and ar-
teries but merely churned sluggishly about in the body
cavity by something we would hardly call a heart.
Above all he has chosen to rely more exclusively than
any other animal on instinct rather than consciousness.
He took one road at a certain now remote junction
while all the rest of us—fishes, reptiles, birds, and mammals—took another. We have been getting further
and further apart ever since.

Many biologists doubt that insects can even feel
pain. Of course no biologist can really know that, and
when I remember how Descartes once convinced half
the world by absolute logic that all creatures except
man were completely insensible, I am not too sure
about the insects. But experiments as well as the ana-
tomical fact that they appear to have no central, all-

controlling brain, support the contention that they have
no total awareness of themselves like that of other
animals. Notoriously, a dragonfly will eat his own
abdomen if it is cut off and presented to him;
notoriously, a male mantis will sometimes go on "making love" after his mate has gnawed his head away.
And what a difference there is between the blank,
staring, compound eye of the most highly developed
insect such as the bee or the wasp and that of the more
human eye of even a frog or a salamander, much less
of the humblest mammal! Could a creature that cannot suffer possibly be "like us"?

That admirable British quarterly *The Countryman*
once incautiously published a communication from a
reader who believed that he had been thanked by a
butterfly. He had noticed on its eye one of the red
parasitic mites which sometimes infest butterflies on
just this organ; he had carefully removed the pest and
then been astonished to have the object of his kindness
uncoil the long hair spring of its proboscis to lick the
hand which had served him. Alas! In the next issue
The Countryman rather shamefacedly published a dry
letter from a less romantic observer who pointed out
that butterflies will often lick the hand of any human
being upon whom they happen to light, presumably
for the salt left by perspiration.

Even without this explanation I doubt that many
readers had been wholly convinced by the first communication. Butterflies happen to be pretty creatures

by our standards and they do lead innocent lives. But the conception of a grateful insect, even a grateful butterfly, is something at which the most amiable imagination boggles. Possibly, as we like to believe, the animals most closely associated with us are capable of that sentiment, but to ask even this is to expect a great deal. Gratitude—as distinguished from a merely graceful attitude of receptivity toward further favors—is a very complex and elaborate feeling. It is in fact, so complex and elaborate that there are some who doubt that even human beings are capable of it and who suspect that it remains an ideal concept, something which some day may be, rather than anything which has so far ever manifested itself in actuality.

The entomologists who have studied the ways of their subjects—as distinguished I mean from those who merely pin bugs on corks and give them names— have usually come, in the end, to regard them with a kind of wondering horror and to realize that their life not only has its seamy side but often appears to have no other. Someone called Henri Fabre "the Insects' Homer" and the phrase has stuck, but though Homer may have hinted some disapproval of certain aspects of his heroes' conduct he certainly did not express the horror which Fabre often did when he contemplated the atrocious mores of certain of the creatures whose private lives he investigated with such passion. "Insects' Ibsen" would be better; "Insects' Zola" or "Insects'

Strindberg" perhaps still nearer the truth; for it is when the scientific naturalist studies these creatures that he most nearly approaches the attitude of the so called "naturalists" among men of letters. The greatest American entomologist William Morton Wheeler, though less eloquent than Fabre, sometimes seems to feel much the same way and even Gustav Eckstein, perhaps the most loving of those who have ever written about the lives of creatures other than man, has told in a remarkable essay how a kind of fear gradually overcame his initial admiration when he contemplated the pullulating vitality of the cockroach.

No one knows how many different kinds of insects there are. New ones are being named, not merely every day, but several times a day; each successive new handbook increases the number which have been classified and notes that there are myriads which have not yet been put on the lists. Within a radius of a few miles of New York City there are thousands, and in the whole world there are some hundreds of thousands which have got names. And whatever the grand total may be there are certainly many times more different sorts of insects than there are different sorts of all the other kinds of animals put together. One despairing taxonomist calculated that if he had begun at the age of twenty to learn the names of twenty-five every day and continued at that rate throughout a normal lifetime he could hardly have hoped to know them all before he dropped into the grave with a new binomial on his lips. Moreover, many species are so successful that the individuals of that species far outnumber the individuals of any other kind of creature. Their way of life is, from the survival standpoint, far more successful than ours. On Lincoln's principle, God must love them more than anything else, though I doubt that he really does.

The idea that these insects are gradually getting the better of us and that they may some day inherit the earth is one with which even the popular mind is familiar—possibly because scientists have themselves raised it, possibly because it is one which even the usually unspeculative mind may have suggested to it in the course of some experience with the attempt to raise flowers or vegetables. But I suspect that the average man would be even more horrified by the possibility than he actually is if he knew more about the manners, customs, and social institutions of these creatures. There are moments when the thought of giving the earth over to the birds, the mammals, or even the Amphibia may seem like a rather good one. Much beauty and much virtue would still be left in the universe. But for the most part the mores of the insects are simply atrocious. It is not merely that they are not humane, they are often very far from being even beastly.

In my own casual and very amateurish way I have watched some of their doings and like most observers, casual or responsible, a good deal of what is not wholly admirable I can accept—perhaps because I have been prepared for it by parallels in human conduct. If a bee wants to work himself to death in the six short weeks of his summer life trying to lay up treasures which he certainly can't take with him, he is only doing what many admired men do, and if the total result for the individual is about one spoonful of honey, I can swallow it quite cheerfully, saying only, "Well, there goes the life work of a bee." If the planners of bee society think it more efficient to have only one fertile female among eighty thousand, leaving all the rest of the females without the enriching experience of a sex life while condemning the one mother to lay something like an egg a minute throughout her adult life, if they think it also a good idea to have the males all drones, one or two of whom will fertilize (only once in her life) a young female while the rest of these males hang uselessly about until frost when the workers will kick them out of the hive to freeze, that also is not really any of my business. The imaginers of human Utopias have also suggested some rather strange ways of life and would be quite capable, I think, of inventing the hive.

For the violence in their lives I am also prepared. The little bombardier beetle who operates from his rear end a sort of poison gas gun which explodes with an audible pop is frankly amusing; the misumnea spiders—crablike in shape and white on white flowers but yellow on yellow ones—who lurk beneath petals

to seize a visiting bee by the nape of the neck and who
hold him thus while they slowly suck out his juices,
are merely practicing one of the arts of the hunter—
they have to live don't they? I do not think that I am
as shocked as Fabre was by what he calls the "savant
brigandage" of certain wasps who have the habit of
paralyzing, but not killing, caterpillars by the hypo-
dermic injection of a poison which will permit the
caterpillar to remain alive and hence unspoiled until
the wasp eggs laid upon it have hatched and the larvae
are ready to eat.

Sometimes when I see another species of caterpillar
slowly dying just before he was ready to make his
cocoon and get the wings he has been looking forward
to, slowly dying because the tiny larvae of a fly whose
mother had inserted eggs under his skin are now
breaking out and will festoon his body with their own
small cocoons; sometimes, on such occasions, I do feel
that he has been played a rather dirty trick. But para-
sitism is part of nature's simple plan and so is what the
biologists call epiparasitism—that is the parasite on the
parasite, and even, I believe, the parasite on the parasite on the parasite. After all, some revolutionary critics
of our society have gone so far as to say that this also
has its parallels in human society. No, what really
revolts me or at least makes me feel that it would
be impossible ever to feel really close to the insects as
I pride myself on feeling close to most other living
creatures, are certain outlandish devices and customs

which would be neither practiced by the unworthy elements in our own society nor ever proposed by those who would radically reform it.

One may, if one likes, raise caterpillars in a cage in order to watch closely the unbelievable process in the course of which the skin splits to reveal the hard chrysalis formed underneath. One may then wait for the butterfly to emerge and slowly expand into their full glory the crumpled wings which look so hopeless when they are first carefully extracted from their case. One may even, if one's taste runs in that direction, keep through the winter the egg case of a mantis until that day in early summer when the literally hundreds of babies stream out, each a miniature replica of its parents, complete with the murderous front arms, the diabolical triangular head, and worst of all, with the fixed determination to carry on their horrible customs, established when even the insects were new, and persisted in stubbornly through millions of years. One may, I say, do all these things. One may cage insects and keep them. But they cannot be made pets of. No two-way communication is possible. We may be aware of them but they are not aware of us—not even as dimly as the salamander or the frog is. They live in some different psychic world, almost, it seems, in some different dimension. Theirs is the ultimate in minding one's own business—such as it is—i.e. the ultimate in the animal's determination not to acknowledge the existence of that intruder, man.

And why, you may ask, should anyone want to hob-nob with a bug? The answer is, I suppose, that I don't really, perhaps that I would rather not. But I do want to realize that I cannot, to strain to the uttermost the possibility of discovering a common ground upon which I and the other creatures may stand. But here the limit has been reached.

Comparatively speaking the frogs and I understand one another perfectly. When I appear he considers whether or not he had better leap into the pond, and he comes to leap less readily as he gets to know me better. The difference between his awareness and that of the dog or cat who understands even some of our words is immense, but perhaps not so great as the difference be-tween the awareness of the frog and the apparently utter obliviousness of the insect.

Between the insects and us there is some fundamen-tal lack of sympathy. Even their adaptations, astonish-ing as they are, seem to us horrible rather than to be admired and their mores, unlike those of other crea-tures, repulsive. When a frog makes love the process may seem a bit cold-blooded but his Venus is unmistak-ably ours. He does not, like the mantis and the spider, get eaten by his wife. He does not, like the tree cricket, discover no better way of escaping this fate than by evolving upon his back a gland which secretes an edi-ble substance which the mate will accept as a substi-tute for his own body. Neither does he, as the wolf spider is sometimes said to do, expect his young to nourish themselves by eating one another while they crawl about on his back. These, I am sure, are devices which neither his kind nor ours would have thought of, even during millions of years. They violate some idea of propriety so fundamental that they would shock a frog as well as a man. And when I realize that I go back to my frogs with the feeling that they and I are not really so different as differences go in this world. I am not sure that even the insects were created on the same two days as the rest of us, or that the God who found both men and frogs good would say as much for them.

CHAPTER 7

NOT AS DUMB AS
YOU THINK

Osa, my black and white cat, produced litter after litter of kittens until everyone—including Osa herself—was sick of the whole business. It has always seemed to me strange that in a world where so many desirable things are scarce there should be an oversupply of anything as delightful as a kitten. But there nearly always is, and so it was now. Osa nursed them for shorter and shorter periods, gave them a more and more sketchy education in tree-climbing and the other fundamentals, began to tell them with a hiss that they were now on their own almost as soon as they could walk. But she went on producing them as frequently as the laws of physiology permit.

Whether this was because, like the hillbilly woman, she never "found out what done it," or simply because, as the case sometimes is with even higher mammals, she was unable to control impulse by discretion, I never knew. In any event she had obviously had more than enough of the joys of motherhood.

Then one morning about dawn she appeared in my wife's bedroom with a single, newborn, unwashed kitten in her mouth. Where she had left the others, if there were any others, we never found out; but she leaped onto the bed, tossed the helpless little lump of wet fur at the startled sleeper, and departed at once, never again to indicate the slightest interest either in the kitten or in the question what had become of it. The line of her reasoning seemed to be something like this: "Apparently you are still interested in these creatures. At least you still act solicitous before they are born and you still coo over them with some show of enthusiasm when they begin to toddle around. All right then, this one is all yours. Look after him if you like. As for me, I am definitely fed up."

Now of course there are a great many students of animal behavior as well as a great many laymen impressed by the authority of these students who will be so outraged by this anecdote that they have probably not read even this far. "This," they have said, "is anthropomorphism (or in plain English, nature-faking) at its most preposterous and worst. Animals don't have a line of reasoning because reasoning is impossible without words and, in fact, consists essentially in muscular contractions at the throat as we silently say the words which constitute what we call thought. The cat, like all animals, behaves because certain motor impulses are the final resultant of a complex of forces involving instincts, conditionings, and impulses stimulated by hormone secretion. Female monkeys deprived of their young will cuddle anything they are given; even male monkeys injected with female hormones will do the same. We can trace every action of your blessed cat in terms of the instincts, the conditions, and the stimuli. We can show you that it had to do just what it did and that the assumption that it had any purpose in mind, or even knew what it was doing, is wholly gratuitous."

Now my objection to this argument is, first of all, that the explanation when given is frightfully complicated and a good deal harder to believe than there is any need for it to be. Granted everything that is known about instinct and conditioning in both the lower animals and the human being it is still easier to account for the behavior of both if one is only willing to admit the intervention in both cases of at least a modicum—larger no doubt for men, smaller for the other animals—of the things called intelligence, will, and purpose. Why on earth should one be so anxious to get rid of them, even at the cost of making our account of behavior exasperatingly more complicated and harder to credit? The brain may be something like a telephone exchange. But somebody uses a telephone to talk over. Doesn't

somebody or something, not the system itself, use a
brain in a similar way?

It is surely a principle of science that the less complicated an hypothesis is the greater preference should be
given it. The Copernican theory replaced the Ptolemaic,
not because it posited a more complicated celestial machine but because it postulated a simpler one. Without
really meaning that my cat Osa said to herself the
words I attributed to her or that she had any "idea" as
clearly formulated as I pretended to believe, it nevertheless remains much easier to account for her behavior
if we grant some intention, however dim, than to deny
it. She had long been "conditioned" to expect from
both my wife and me some aid and emotional participation in connection with her numerous accouchements.
But as in all similar cases the chain of causes which
leads from past experience to present action is shorter,
simpler, and clearer if we assume for the animals, as all
except the most absolute behaviorists assume for our
own kind, the intervention of something which involves
consciousness and purpose in some degree.

Often enough it has been claimed that the whole behavior of an animal throughout its entire existence can
"be accounted for" without the necessity of invoking at
any point the hypothesis of consciousness. Somewhat
less frequently the same claim has been made concerning human behavior, and in this case the conclusion
drawn is not indeed that human consciousness does not

exist but that it is a mere passive epiphenomenon which plays no active role, and might conceivably disappear without affecting in the slightest the observable behavior of a human being. But even if for the sake of argument we grant the claim, we nevertheless do know by direct evidence that in our own individual case the consciousness does exist and that it happens to be real whether or not we should, in the absence of direct evidence, be compelled to assume it.

Of course each of us could say, "The only consciousness which I can be sure about is my own. Possibly it is the only one in the entire universe and possibly all my fellow creatures perform acts similar to mine without being gifted with that awareness which, so I am told, is not necessary to explain their actions." But we do not usually say this to ourselves; we usually assume as more probable the contrary—namely, that the other creatures who behave much as we do are similarly aware of what they are doing. And if we do make that assumption, then we have only slightly less reason for making a similar one about the animals, who appear almost as indubitably happy or miserable as human beings do, and thus make the hypothesis that they are unaware only slightly less wildly improbable than the parallel possibility that no one except our individual self either knows what he does or is aware of emotional concomitants to his doing. Perhaps Pavlov's dogs do not have to know that they are hungry; perhaps they would behave exactly as they do if they did not. But the most reasonable assumption would seem to be that they do know it, even as you and I.

Nature-faking is possible in either direction and it need be no more conscious or intentional in the one case than in the other. Often it is not a question of how like or unlike the conscious concomitants of behavior in animals and human beings are *proved* to be but simply a question of the assumptions made. Nowadays, moreover, the scientist is very much prejudiced in favor of mechanism even when dealing with man so that it is no wonder if he goes as far as possible in that direction when dealing with animals who cannot, like his human subjects, object with a "But see here, old man, I know I am conscious whether you do or not, and no matter how fully you think you have 'accounted for me' in terms of reflexes, I happen to know from direct experience that the 'unnecessary hypothesis' of consciousness happens to be a true one."

I open at random a book written for popular consumption by the Professor of Natural History at one of the great British universities. It has a chapter on bird song and this chapter begins with a description of a man singing in the bath. This, says the author, is generally agreed to be an expression of the joy of life and of good will toward men on the part of the bather. "But what has the song of the bath to do with the song of birds? Absolutely nothing! That is why I mention it, to warn you of its danger, because we are inclined, almost unconsciously, to interpret the songs of birds and other creatures from our own experience, and to look upon them as expressions of the joy of living, since they sometimes play that role with us."

He then goes on to say that we have no right to make this assumption and he proceeds to prove that the real meaning of bird song is utilitarian, that it functions chiefly as a warning to other birds of the singer's intention to defend his right to a certain territory. This, he continues, is the only thing which can be proved and, therefore, the only thing we should be willing to believe.

But suppose we judged human music and its performers in the same way. Suppose you had heard at the opera some justly famous prima donna singing "Voi che sapete" from Don Giovanni or even Mary Martin washing that man out of her hair. You have assumed that the one genuinely loves music and experiences some emotion related to that which Mozart's aria expresses, also that the other in some sense enjoys her performance. But a scientist of another kind—an economist— comes along and says, "I have studied the evidence. I find that in both cases the performer really sings for so many thousand dollars per week. In fact she won't sing in public unless she is paid quite a large sum. This proves that what sentimentalists like to think of as something called 'the aesthetic experience' is mere moonshine. *You* may sing in the bath because you are happy and like to do it. But so far, at least, as professional singers are concerned, they sing for nothing but money."

The fallacy—and it is the fallacy in an appalling number of psychological, sociological, and economic "interpretations" of human behavior—is, of course, the fallacy of the "nothing but." Actually it is perfectly possible to make a living by singing and still, in a very meaningful sense, to enjoy doing it. Nearly everything which is done well is done from motives which are at least mixed. And there is nothing in human experience or knowledge to make it seem unlikely that the cardinal announcing from the branch of a tree his claim on a certain territory is not also terribly glad to be doing it, very joyous in his realization of his own vigor and artistry. Mr. Carl Sandburg's fish pedlar was. Why not an opera singer or a bird? "He rejoiceth as a strong man to run a race." That, or Plato's remark that we take pleasuring in doing whatever we do well, sheds more light on the psychology of human beings than most of what is found in textbooks of psychology. And there is at least as much reason for believing as there is for doubting that it applies to animals too.

Given, as we are, the choice between believing that all nature to some extent participates in the joy of life and believing that except for us—if indeed we are an exception—all living things are as dead as machines, I cannot see how anyone who does not hate life itself can hesitate over his choice. Whoever listens to a bird song and says, "I do not believe there is any joy in it" has not proved anything about birds. But he has revealed a good deal about himself. Moreover, an age like ours which, on the whole, not only says this but persistently and consistently says the same sort of thing about all the activities, human or animal, which it undertakes to "interpret," reveals a good deal about its own ruling spirit.

Of a certain seventeenth-century mechanist who, like some of his present day descendants, got rid of mysteries by means of explanations harder to credit than the mysteries themselves, it was said that "He could believe anything provided only it was *not* in the Bible." Even today it seems too little realized that "wishful thinking" works both ways and that one need not necessarily assume implacable detachment on the part of, say, a mechanist and a materialist while taking it for granted that his opponents are obviously moved by the desire to defend prejudice, childhood beliefs, inherited religion, or the economic consequences of a belief in God. It is just as possible to *want* to believe that man is a machine and animals incapable of thought as it is to *want* to believe that both were created by the hand of God in 4004 B.C.

Moreover, it is plain enough that the extent to which an individual is willing to grant understanding and feeling to animals very often depends upon the nature of his relations with them. If the scientist who knows them only in the inhuman atmosphere of the laboratory is most likely to think of them as machines, the keeper of pets is no less likely to indulge in the wildest overinterpretation of their behavior. Theodore Roosevelt was the obstreperous enemy of nature-faking, but Theodore Roosevelt was also a mighty hunter who liked to shoot almost anything which could be called alive and he was, therefore, a person to whom the assumption that an elephant would prefer life to the honor of becoming a Presidential trophy was naturally unwelcome.

Those of us who lean in the opposite direction, who always tend, as it were, to give the animals the benefit of the doubt in the matter of understanding and sensibility, may also be influenced by the nature of our desires. But we have, nevertheless, one pragmatic argument on our side. We are doing ourselves a favor, or rather, we are guarding our own rights, because of a curious fact which seems obvious enough but which I do not remember ever to have seen stated. It is simply this: *Man has never denied anything of the animals without coming, shortly thereafter, to deny it of himself also.*

To begin with the theologians denied that the animals had souls. Undoubtedly the intention was to exalt man at the animal's expense, but the result, after a few centuries, was the conclusion that man did not have one either, since what could not be demonstrated in the beast was equally undemonstrable in him. Reason, of which man alone was assumed to be capable, still remained and it was carefully distinguished from such mental

process as the animals were supposed capable of. But
the result soon was that man's own sovereign reason was
more and more encroached upon by the rôles assigned
to those instincts and conditioned reflexes shared with
animals until many began to doubt whether "pure reason" was not as much a myth as the soul had proved
to be. Behaviorism—the theory that animal behavior
can best be studied and can be wholly accounted
for without assuming the intervention of either reason,
purpose, or will—leads even more promptly to the conclusion that human behavior can be studied in the same
way and that what we had formerly supposed to be the
most significant aspect of our being, namely, consciousness, is a mere epiphenomenon, a sort of by-product of
behavior, which plays no real rôle in our conduct. Descartes believed that all animals acted, as one of his
disciples put it, like a watch and by merely mechanical
means. The intention was to make an absolute distinction between them and man. But the way was prepared
for the conclusion that man also is mechanical. By trying to establish man's exclusive possession of a soul he
actually succeeded only in depriving him of it.

Thus it has somehow or other regularly turned out
that what we refuse to share with our fellow creatures
we ultimately deny ourselves and that whenever we try
to believe ourselves too much more than an animal we
lessen ourselves as well as them. The conclusion that we
are very much alike forces itself upon us so inescapa-
bly that we can only exalt or even respect ourselves if

we respect them also. I shall continue to believe that Osa's actions had some conscious and at least dimly purposeful accompaniment, because if I do not then someone is bound to prove that I never really know what I am doing either.

Nearly everyone who has ever read Montaigne remembers the famous passage in which he tells how he was dutifully amusing his kitten when he was struck with a curious thought. Perhaps the kitten, no less dutiful than he, was amusing him. Those who have had much experience with kittens are not likely to suppose this possibility a very probable one. Such well meant confusions in which everyone is nobly sacrificing himself to everyone else are probably among the things which only human beings are permitted to achieve. But Montaigne, who did not himself take this particular speculation too seriously, was registering another of his famous firsts. Did anyone before his time ever try in quite that freely speculative way to put himself in an animal's place? Some had thoughtlessly taken for granted that man and beast think and feel in identical ways; others had thoughtlessly taken it for granted that the beasts had no mental or psychic life worth considering. The Egyptians once knew that cats were gods; Descartes was soon to know that they were pure machines. But Montaigne was wondering what it would be like to be a cat. He was being acutely aware of that gulf across which there is no clear communication and of which, for that very reason, we cannot know the breadth. He was realizing how we share the world with many different creatures, some of whom are in many ways embarrassingly like ourselves, but that we do not know either how to take them or how we should behave toward them because, for all we may confidently assert about their capacities or their limitations, we cannot really have even the dimmest conception of the most important thing about them—namely, in what kind of awareness they have their being.

We have made them, in so far as we were able, serve our purposes. We have also anatomized and classified them into hundreds of thousands of species of each of which we keep records and specimens in vast museums as though some awful calamity would fall upon us if one got confused with another. Yet for all this and for all the possibly more hopeful observation of their behavior, it is still possible for some to believe that they are little more than machines, others that they are at least not much more machine-like than we are. Most of us vacillate between two opposite extremes. We may think we believe one thing and then find ourselves in something like Montaigne's situation.

Take, for instance, the case of Samuel Johnson who was not a man given to cultivating whimseys. Boswell is, nevertheless, authority for the statement that Johnson seemed to feel that he had made a gaffe when he remarked in Hodge's presence that Hodge was not as fine as certain other cats he had had. Such extravagances do not mean that those of us who are guilty of them really believe what they seem to imply. But they do mean that we are so aware of our ignorance that we are taking no chances. We believe that a cat might be hurt by an untactful remark to just about the extent that we believe spilling salt is unlucky. And we do throw some over our shoulders.

Every age applies to the eternally unsolvable mysteries the techniques to which it has become newly addicted. In connection with that fact I have always remembered the indignation of an officer of the Rationalist Press Association, that still-standing pillar of Victorian scepticism, when he told me that he could have predicted that this age would turn up with a statistical proof of the existence of God and that it was this to which Professor Rhine's experiments with extrasensory perception really come down. Some ages, he said, put their trust in metaphysics and come up with a logical demonstration. Some believe in the authority of the inner light or the power which the imagination has to make contact with truth, and they are accordingly blessed with intimations of immortality. But now when government and business alike put their faith in polls or charts, when even physics abandons immutable physical law in favor of the statistical probability which alone enables us to predict how matter will behave, it has become inevitable that God should manifest himself in the same way. He is not proved by a syllogism and He does not announce himself to the transcendental imagination which has tuned in on the infinite. But He does enable a sensitive person to guess right somewhat more often than He would in a world ruled by nothing except chance.

You may, concluded my Rationalist acquaintance, deny that you are calling it God. But it comes down to the same thing. By demonstrating an irrational element you are leaving a back door invitingly open. And in the end the statistical proof of God will go the way of the metaphysical and the intuitive. The arguments will still be there, but somehow they will cease to carry conviction. And presently some new way of penetrating the impenetrable will come, for a time, into fashion.

Now I do not quite go along with my Rationalist friend, but for reasons analogous to his I do hold it inevitable that our generation should apply to the lesser mystery of the animal psyche its new-found toy, the Intelligence Test. That test was supposed to give us for the first time in history a reliable way of measuring men from the cradle to the grave. It labeled us immutably "Grade A" or "Grade C." To the infant just beginning to toddle it set the bounds to his hope. "Thus far shalt thou go and no further. It took you too long to put the triangular block into the triangular hole. You are doomed to be forever inferior." Why not, someone inevitably asked, use the same infallible method to end all speculation about the animal mind and to settle once and for all the question how smart our fellow creatures are?

More than a generation ago Edward Thorndike built

his first mazes. Since that time scores of scientists have been busy amusing themselves by setting problems for the animals to solve and coming to the gratifying conclusion that we are lots smarter than any of them, except maybe the apes. Moreover, and less happily, most of man's own particular favorites come out very badly indeed. The dog does go well ahead of the cat and that will please most people. But man's best friend himself does not show up very well, and the horse, which Buffon called the noblest of the animals, is little better than a moron. The donkey is a genius by comparison; in fact he and the pig stand just about at the head of the class if we assume that the monkeys, being only somewhat lesser men rather than animals, are *hors concours*.

The brightest of the latter are so close to us that it becomes positively embarrassing. It is proved that by the definition we have been pleased to set up that we and they alone are indubitably capable of reason as opposed to mere learning by trial and error. Only we and they can legitimately solve, rather than blunder through, a problem. But the apes can do more than that. One superingenious experimenter taught them the value of money by using chips of different colors as rewards for effort and then providing slot machines on which the chips could be spent for goodies of various kinds. Not only did his charges work gladly for chips; not only did they learn to distinguish the various denominations; they also exhibited personality differences, some revealing themselves as misers, some as spendthrifts who squandered their money on bananas and grapes as soon as they got it. Moreover, the profit motive was strong in all of them, and it is hence obvious that when the time comes for us to make the shift from our present economy to that of the nonacquisitive society there will be a problem we had not counted on: apes as well as men are going to need re-education.

But what of the truly lower animals whom many of us have learned to love and to whom we have sometimes felt very close? What of the not too bright dog, the even less intelligent cat, and the indubitably moronic horse? Must we henceforth think of them only as we think of some idiot child to whom nothing but duty (aided perhaps by pity) can attach us? Is the fellowship we seem sometimes to enjoy a pure delusion? Or is it possible that there is a catch somewhere, that the relative slowness of a dog or cat in learning to find his way out of a laboratory maze is not a fully adequate measure of his whole mind and spirit?

Some of the brighter experimenters have occasionally had fleeting doubts about the validity, not of the whole enterprise, but at least of some of the details of their method. One was, for example, mildly disturbed to discover that by the maze test—and the maze is the most widely employed device—rats were proved to be just three times as intelligent as college freshmen. Overlooking an obvious opportunity for cynicism, he concluded that this particular test was not, by itself, completely trustworthy. But it does seem that one might go even a

little further. Unless rats really are three times as intelligent as freshmen then there is no sound reason for
believing that the maze test is of any more value in
comparing the intelligence of a cat with the intelligence
of a dog than it is for comparing that of a rat and a
man. When you have learned that one memorizes the
turnings of a road faster than the other, you have
learned that he does indeed learn these turnings faster.
But it is certainly not clear that you have learned anything else at all.

Let us skip as too obvious for comment the fact that
an animal is not in a position to do his best when he is
kept in a laboratory cage and set problems which he has
perhaps only an inadequate reason for wanting to solve.
To judge him by what he there accomplishes is about
as fair as it would be to judge a human being by his
showing on an examination administered for a purpose he does not understand while he is being imprisoned for a crime of whose nature he is ignorant and
the possible penalty for which he cannot know. It is in
other words a thoroughly Kafkaesque situation.

But having skipped all that, let us consider the fact
that the animal is also being judged by his ability to
solve puzzles of the special sort that man has found
himself good at, and that in a word the very definition
of intelligence is one which man has devised to favor
himself. If the beaver (a stupid animal, so they say),
the lynx or, for that matter, the dog or the cat were to
set the definitions and make the tests, it might well turn

out that man showed up pretty badly when attempting
the things which the dog or the cat could do well. How
good are you at following a rabbit's scent or finding
your way home when lost? How sure are you that the
ability to do those things has less to do with the abstrac-
tion called intelligence than the ability to thread an artificial maze?

Suppose that the mathematicians in our society somehow got the prestige and authority which would entitle
them to maintain that the ability to solve mathematical
problems was the real test of intelligence, or of whatever you want to call "the highest manifestations of the
mind?" Suppose that you were then summoned before
one of the mathematicians, promised a sugar plum or at
least a pat on the head whenever you did well, and then
presented with a series of problems beginning, let us
say, with a pair of simultaneous quadratics and ending
with a rather tough differential equation. Suppose on the
basis of your possibly poor showing you were classified
as quite appallingly stupid, and suppose the mathematical master went on to conclude, not merely that you
were not in any way intelligent, but also that, for this
reason, you were obviously little capable of deep feeling
and that only "sentimentalists" would consider it very
important whether or not you were given much consideration in the management of the society.

Under such circumstances you would certainly
protest that whatever the importance or beauty of
mathematical reasoning might be, some of your best,

dearest, most interesting, and most charming friends
were so far from being able to solve a differential equation that they would probably find it impossible to
understand what one is. You would further protest that
the power to solve problems of this sort, like a talent
for chess, is so far from being a reliable guide to intelligence of other kinds that one might well be intimately
acquainted with an individual without having the
slightest reason for supposing that he either was or was
not gifted with the special kind of insight which enables
some people to see at once just where it is worth while
to pull at a tangled knot or a differential equation. To
apply analogous tests and to draw from them the conclusions which have sometimes been drawn calls to mind
a statement made by the late Will Cuppy: "Frogs will
eat red-flannel worms fed to them by biologists. This
proves a great deal about both parties concerned."

One thing seems certain. The animals may exhibit little intelligence and all of them, except the apes, may be
incapable of logical processes. Their lives may be, if
you want to put it this way, radically thoughtless. But
there is nothing they are less like than a mentally de-
fective person. Hebephrenia, that all pervasive, dull
sluggishness which characterizes human unfortunates de-
ficient in normal powers, is the exact opposite of the
mental state they seem to exhibit. Many of them are
vivacious as no man ever is. Watching them at work or
play one often feels that they are more vividly alive
than we ever are.

Notoriously, their senses are alert to a degree hard for us to imagine, and such sensual alertness seems to imply some correspondingly tingling awareness. Common sense long ago rejected Descartes' monstrous and gratuitous insistence that an animal, being a machine without a soul, could not possibly, even when screaming in agony, be feeling anything at all. But unless one is prepared to accept that thesis, it is difficult to see how one can deny that the dog, apparently beside himself at the prospect of a walk with his master, is experiencing a joy the intensity of which it is beyond our power to imagine much less to share. In the same way his dejection can at least appear to be no less bottomless. Perhaps the kind of thought of which we are capable dims both our sensual and our emotional lives at the same time that it makes us less victims of either. Was any man, one wonders, ever as dejected as a lost dog? Perhaps certain of the animals can be both more joyful and more utterly desolate than any man ever was.

"We look before and after and pine for what is not." That fact was thus phrased in order to claim for us the privilege of a uniquely agonizing unhappiness. But is the claim really justified, does the knowledge that a past was and that a future will be add to or detract from the importance of the moment? Is sorrow's crown of sorrows the remembrance of happier things or could it be rather the inability to remember that happiness ever was or could be? The animals woe—no less truly, perhaps, the animal's happiness—is unqualified by either

memory or anticipation. It is a fact which fills for him
the whole universe. He knows nothing of the consola-
tions of either religion or philosophy. He cannot even
say, "This also will pass." Every moment is his eternity
because he cannot know that it will not last forever. If,
therefore, his joy is without shadow, perhaps his being
in misery is without alleviation. And that, so some
might say, is what hell would be like. What other creature has ever been so miserable as an animal who has
never known anything except want and abuse, and who
cannot know that such a thing as kindness or even comfort exists in the universe?

For a long time now one of the most popular magazines has been publishing a continuing series of anecdotes
illustrating the intelligence and wisdom of animals, both
wild and domestic. These anecdotes are contributed by
readers; there is no evidence that any check is made
upon either the competence or even the veracity of the
observers, and a good many of the tales are tall indeed.
The only thing, I am afraid, that they really prove is
simply that even in this rather too scientific age a great
many people want very much to believe what their
primitive ancestors took for granted—namely, that the
consciousness of the beast is not essentially different
from our own.

This it seems to me is at least an amiable weakness
and reveals a kind of generosity of spirit very different
from the arrogance of most laboratory scientists, who

seem bent on demonstrating their own high endowments by demonstrating the absence of these endowments in all creatures except themselves. And it is odd that the two tendencies should coexist, with the laboratory scientist often defeating his own purpose by the grotesque inappropriateness of his experiments, while a great public eagerly accepts on the scantiest of evidence what sometimes sounds like a mere modernized excerpt from one of the once popular beast epics. Perhaps there is no connection between the two phenomena, but it would be pleasant to believe that the second is a reaction against the solemn absurdity of some of the mental testers who have posed the most preposterous problems and come up with the most preposterous conclusions. To answer nonsense of one kind with nonsense of an opposite sort seems frequently to have been the best the human race could do in the way of redressing a balance.

CHAPTER 8

PRESIDING OVER A VACUUM

One of my city friends—and friend I still call him—
has a word for what I do when I get away to Connecticut. He likes to picture me motionless in some sort of a
swami squat before an ant hill or a dandelion and en-
gaged in what he calls "presiding over a vacuum."

This friend is not one of your passionate haters of
nature. Indeed he rather prides himself upon being able
to take a bird or leave it. He does not, like the famous
Mrs. Bell of Boston, request acquaintances country-
bound to "kick a tree for me." But he does hold that

you can't think unless you have something to think *about* and he suspects me of deliberately losing myself in "the intense inane"—the last word being taken in the more usual, less favorable sense. For botany, bird-watching, and tadpole-collecting he can summon up a certain tolerance. These are processes. But like a good eighteenth-century disciple of John Locke he holds that you cannot possibly be in a position to take anything out of your head unless you first put something into it. And he is convinced that from the vacuum—which some call contemplation—there is nothing which can be taken.

Now what he regards as a chronic and inevitable state of affairs certainly does sometimes present itself as an incidental difficulty. Just as the writer who has stared fruitlessly at the typewriter for an hour may get a brilliant idea while shaving, so one often sees nothing while one is searching the depths for it and then, while doing something quite prosaic, one may catch out of the corner of the eye a glimpse into what seems like the heart of things. The final end of man may be, as Aristotle and I firmly believe, contemplation. But man is still too short a way along the road which leads from the acting animal to the contemplative one to be able very often to go deliberately about his real business. Usually he must consciously *do* something, even though it is only in the hope that this doing will hypnotize him into the state which makes contemplation possible.

It is this fact which explains the keeping of records, the listing of birds, the pressing of flowers, even the harmless routine of the thermometer commonly practiced even by those least aware of the world about them. We do not really care whether it is ninety or ninety-one, four above or five below. But we do hope that in the process of discovering what the mercury reads we may be made aware of heat or cold, of the fact that summer and winter are knowable realities. No doubt this same fact explains other paradoxes also: the paradox of the hunters who sometimes really do love the animals they slaughter and have merely never learned any method of making contact other than that of killing the thing they love. Some men, said Thoreau, go on to the end of their lives still believing that catching fish is the real reason for fishing, and he might have noted the even more remarkable fact that others, having reached a realization of what it is they are looking for, lose it again in their absorption with the methods. Reading the thermometer or classifying the reptiles comes to seem an end in itself, and the museum scientists find themselves doggedly separating subspecies in basement laboratories because they had once wanted to see what was going on in the world. Thus, so I have been told, saints who have lost the mystic vision desperately reiterate the formulae of prayer throughout the night of the soul.

Sometimes the method works and sometimes it does not. Similarly, I suppose, the hunter sometimes realizes

suddenly what it is that he is hunting, and sometimes
the scientist, trying perhaps to decide whether or not
the leaf of some specimen of a weed really is sufficiently more hairy than the type specimen to justify him
in recording it as a variety, suddenly catches sight of
the gleam which first led him down his dark alley. And
if I, less busy, sometimes find myself presiding over a
vacuum, that vacuum sometimes becomes suddenly mi-
raculously full.

It is not that I learn many lessons on the how-doth-
the-little-busy-bee level of profundity. I am not aware
that observation of the ant has ever made me less a
sluggard or that, in general, the maxims most often deduced from the examples supposed to be set us by the
animals are usually either very convincingly deduced or
very useful so far as the practical everyday business of
living is concerned. Fabre lamented at some length the
bad moral effect produced upon the whole French na-
tion by the ungenerous spirit of La Fontaine's version of
the grasshopper-ant fable, and it has often occurred to
me that the bee who works himself to death in a few
weeks gathering honey which neither he nor his fellows
could possibly use up if man did not take it away from
him is less a model for imitation than a warning to "the
worker": do not permit yourselves, comrades, to be victims of exploitation.

The less specific the moral drawn from the behavior
of the beasts, the less obviously does it seem false.
When Whitman admires them because

They do not sweat and whine about their condition,
They do not lie awake in the dark and weep for their sins,
They do not make me sick discussing their duty to God,

that seems at least to be true. Courage they do seem to
teach us and if they are not quite incapable of lamenta-
tion there does not seem to be much in the universe except man that tends to make a specialty of it. But even
that lesson can be learned—if it can be learned at all
—not so much by observation or by speculation as by a
kind of contemplative participation. Our fellow creatures did not themselves learn their vast patience and
they do not know how they practice it. In a sense that
patience does not really exist as patience except in so
far as we are aware of it. But to be, if one can, aware,
is to profit by it as perhaps nothing else in the universe
can.

Except for man, every living creature is active, principally if not exclusively. It is not even certain that the
cat, dozing by the fire, is as contemplative as he looks;
and the animal psychologists are perhaps right when
they tell us that a dog's world is a world of sounds and
smells, not a world of ideas. Below the level of such
creatures, down in the dim world of budding plants and
quietly multiplying shellfish is something which would
perhaps exist in no consciousness at all if it did not exist
in ours. By being aware of it we do for it what it cannot do for itself: we give it being as well as mere existence.

Until the invention of the microscope, the beautiful

traceries on the glass shells of a billion billion diatoms had no such being and that fact is easy to grasp—nothing had ever seen them. But neither, in one sense, does anything in the natural world achieve more than a relatively dim being until we confer that being upon it. He, therefore, who takes the trouble to look at a weed blooming by the road side has rescued it from nothingness. He has given it a place in some consciousness and until something did that, there was one realm at least in which it was only potential.

So at least it must seem to those who are unable to feel sure that there is in the universe anything else very much like our own awareness. If there is a God who made things for His delight rather than for ours, then perhaps it makes no difference to anything except ourselves whether we contemplate the universe or not. Perhaps even, in that case, we too should merely exist and act and thus contribute to the spectacle existing for a mind little interested in our own feeble contributions to an already perfect consciousness. But unless we are very sure that such a perfect awareness does exist, we ought to do our best to be conscious of a world which otherwise nothing might ever be conscious of.

Perhaps, indeed, that is the most important of all the things we are capable of, perhaps it is the true end of man. Some of the theologians of the seventeeth century came close to thinking so when they protested against the naïver notion that the world had been made merely for our *use* and insisted, as I am suggesting, that it was on the contrary made for our admiration, as a sort of demonstration of what the Creator is capable of. It was Francis Bacon who popularized the newer utilitarianism, and he is generally credited with the first effective formulation of the assumption that the control rather than the contemplation of nature is the principal business of man. But it still may be truer to say, as a much later philosopher did, that "This curious world which we inhabit is more wonderful than it is convenient; more beautiful than it is useful; it is more to be admired and enjoyed than used."

We know or think we know a great deal about making it useful or at least convenient. That is the business of the technicians, and ours is a society in which the technician rules. How to see it as beautiful—and that is the same thing as how to enjoy it—is or at least once was the business of the poet and the philosopher, both of whom have now come to seem to most, merely ignorant and unsuccessful technicians, unfortunates who bear the same relation to the scientist and the sociologist as the astrologer and the alchemist bore to the astronomer and the chemist. But that is perhaps the reason why the world, which grows constantly more convenient, certainly does not seem to most of those who live in it either more beautiful or, they fear, more enjoyable.

Poetry, like all the other arts, is an aid to contemplation and subtler than the routine of the thermometer or the classification of butterflies. But like the other aids it also may become an end in itself, and the "lover of

poetry" is frequently one who loves nothing except the
mechanics of an incantation which no longer calls anything forth from the vasty deep and who therefore
spends his time, not presiding over a vacuum, but por-
ing over what has become no more than gibberish. No
good ode to a skylark was ever intended as a permanent substitute for the skylark himself, and yet it is common enough to find admirers of the "nature poets" rather proud of the fact that they have never looked at a
bird and certainly could not tell Wordsworth's Lesser
Celandine from Tennyson's dozing Pimpernel. They
know how the poets talk but not what they talk about.

In the classroom a student who had been reading
Keats once asked if there were any nightingales in the
United States and was laughed at for his pains—not because any other member of the group knew but because
it was thought ridiculous to raise a question so remote
from the poem. Perhaps there are college courses in the
romantic poets which include some discussion of the
birds, beasts, and flowers with which these poets were so
strangely familiar, but I never heard of one. Yet I can
think of "background materials" sometimes presented
which seem to me less immediately relevant, and I
should not be shocked to find in a college catalogue
something like "English B237. Natural History for
English Majors."

"Up, up and quit your books" is not an adjuration
commonly thought advisable in universities, but there
are occasions—as, for instance, when studying Words-

worth—when it might be advisable. Commonly the professor who has just finished an exposition of the poem concludes somewhat as follows: "The assignment for next time is the next twenty pages of your anthology and don't forget that the monthly book report is due." Is it any wonder that students don't take poetry seriously?

All men are Peter Bell most of the time. When a yellow primrose becomes for the scientist more than simply a yellow primrose, it is likely to be merely *Primula* sp. and that is no great advance. For the student of literature it probably remains stubbornly "A poem in four-line stanzas of iambic pentameter by William Wordsworth (1770-1850)." What's *Primula* to him or he to *Primula*? But sometimes the answer does come: "Everything."

Not all the techniques together—science, poetry, and mere looking—have ever yet enabled anyone even at his happiest moments to confer being even for one instant on more than a small fragment of all that exists. What we should like to do—though it might blast us if we did—is to realize the sum of the earth's energy and joy. The most we can usually do is to participate in the opening of one flower or in a rabbit's running of his race. There is too much beauty and too much joy for us to take in. Any man really capable of what at moments he feels himself on the brink of would be conscious of everything going on in the universe. He would be both flying with the eagle and growing with the grass. Perhaps in that case he would also be God.

CHAPTER 9

THE MICROSCOPIC EYE

The house in which I live is what some people would call "shut in." It is on a not much traveled road near the top of a hill, but there are higher hills round about and there is not much "view."

That is the way I like it, and this, I suppose, is one of the signs that I belong to that class called introverts, of whom the wake-up-and-live psychologists so sharply disapprove. Many of us, however, are not particularly sorry for ourselves, and some of these psychologists would be surprised at how much satisfaction we take in things which would not suit them at all. We do not mind being shut in if we can choose the people and the things we are shut in with.

Too long a view in either time or space makes people miss a great deal that is close at hand, and it is my experience that those who are quickly bored in the country are usually those who lack "the microscopic eye," those to whom "nature" means only "scenery," and "scenery" means only "views." Charles Lamb once declared that he would not much care if he never saw another mountain, and, while I would not by any means go so far, I think I know what he meant. To know nature only that way is like knowing a city only by its skyline. To feel the life of either city or country, one must be actually in it, aware of the excitement and variety of individual lives. People are often blamed because they cannot see the wood for the trees, but that does not seem to me so bad as not seeing the trees for the wood.

Summer especially is a time for the short view. In winter not so much is going on, and by way of compensation the large forms of trees and hills are revealed in all their beautiful nakedness. But summer is too fully clothed to reveal form on this scale. The trees are muffled in leaves, the outline of one merges into that of the other, and they combine to blur the shapes of the earth itself. For form one must now look closely— at the individual leaf or flower in front of one's eyes, or at the shoot coming up out of the ground.

A few years before the most recent world war, a fanatical German published a typically German book of startling photographs called *Urformen der Kunst*. Its thesis was that all man's conceptions of abstract form, whether architectural, structural, or decorative, came from the natural forms of stems, buds, and seed pods. His magnified images were startlingly effective and even if one is not willing to follow him all the way, one thing is certain. To whatever extent man has copied nature's inventions in his own building, it is the detail of plants that he has copied. Art can do little with a landscape except to reproduce a somewhat schematized image of it. The grand forms of hill and valley offer no hints to the architect or the designer. He cannot build as the earth is built; nor is there in hill and valley any formal design which he can copy.

Landscape is not inclined to geometry. The human mind is; most living things are. They employ, as man does, the circle, the sphere, the triangle, and the star. Tree and herb alike demonstrate how stresses may be calculated and supported by struts, buttresses, and columns like those which man will use. Also, and unlike the hill or the valley, they reveal how regularity and repetition constitute the essential elements of formal design. If we did not borrow from living nature a very large part of the art of both building and design, then we, being also living things, independently discovered what the builders of branches, the designers of seed pods, the constructors of shells and bones, discovered before us. And it is all this which passes unnoticed in the mere general view.

That cult of the sublime which developed in the

eighteenth century, and which is generally credited with the creation of the great body of romantic nature-poetry, was, I am convinced, an enemy of another kind of appreciation of nature which means more to me. For this cult focused attention on landscape, and encouraged a mere vague ecstasy, whose devotees, instead of really examining nature, projected upon her their own fancies. Mountains served chiefly the purpose served by the crystal ball of the pseudo-seer or the glittering speculum of the hypnotist. Those who gazed upon them went into a sort of trance, which may have helped to bring out something in them, but discovered nothing outside themselves. If nature is to be learned from, she must be known, and to be known she must be looked at. Your Wordsworthians hated naturalists because they were afraid the naturalist might take them out of themselves and show them something they did not want to see.

Even an amateur like myself will seldom lack something to see if he will only look. "Lift up thine eyes unto the hills" is a religious exhortation. "Go to the ant, thou sluggard," is a scientific one. And, at least for certain temperaments, it is the more fruitful. Because I obey it, the place where I am is never really the same place two days in succession, and I can take every morning the same short walk down a certain wood road because it is not really the same walk.

Certain things, to be sure, repeat themselves with the

seasons. One morning in autumn there are shooting crystals of ice in a puddle where before there was only water; one morning in spring there will be water where
for long months there has been only the glassy ice. But
from that morning on, hardly a day will pass when
some old friend is not to be greeted anew. Even the
most casual observers are seldom unaware of the unrolling of the ferns—partly because they come early, before
there is any lush undergrowth, and partly because they
are so striking in themselves. "Fiddle-backs" they are
commonly and inevitably called, and no doubt the curl
on the end of the neck of the modern violin was copied
from them. But the Ionic capital also either copies or
reinvents that spiral unrolling, and the emerging form
is one of the most obvious of the *Urformen der Kunst*.

So, too, are the reinforced columnar fruiting stems of
the equisetum, or horsetail, which push up at about the
same time, though not in the same place. For the equisetum prefers stony ground, and around here it thrusts
itself upward with astonishing force through the com-
pact tar and gravel at the edge of my hard-surfaced
road. Fairly early, too, I look for the queer shaped
flowers of what the delicate call wood betony and the
downright call lousewort. Last of all, and writing finis
to the season—possibly after frost has already come—
the yellow flowers of the witch hazel break out unex-
pectedly. Perhaps, though I do not know, the "witch"
part was first suggested by this perverse blooming habit.
It seems as dangerously abnormal as the crowing hen

who was once thought to have given her soul to the devil.

Some things grow fast and some grow slowly. The puff ball rounds itself out to melon size almost overnight, and the huge yellow mass of the gelatinous fungus which attacks rotten wood is suddenly there where it wasn't the last time one passed by. At the other extreme are the lichens, sometimes a foot in diameter on a boulder, and yet, to the eye, precisely the same size for five years on end. Some say that certain giant individuals of this family must have lived through whole millenniums, and that it is they, rather than the redwoods of our western coast, which are the oldest living things on earth. Once when I was arranging a terrarium to remind me during the long winter months what summer is like, I spent a good deal of time searching for a lichen on a smallish stone before my dull mind realized that I was asking for the impossible. Only a boulder or slab heavy enough to stay put for many years on end can acquire a lichen large enough to be noticed. Moss grows rather quickly, and what a rolling stone really can't gather is lichens.

But not everything is regularly recurrent along this same half-mile stretch of wood road. Last autumn, for example, a certain low bank covered with leaf-mold was star-scattered for the first time with the curious mushroom called Geaster, a kind of puff ball whose outer skin splits into petal-like segments which reflex until they form a five-pointed star with a round button in the middle—another striking example of nature's decorative use of geometrical design. I have now seen them once, but there are other queer things which I have never come across. For years I have poked hopefully at rotting logs (and found a great many surprising things in them), but I have never come across myxomycete, one of the puzzles and paradoxes of the natural world, which is said not to be uncommon. A mobile film of jelly often several inches square, it is (so the books say) neither plant nor animal, neither a colony nor an individual. It flows along like an amoeba, but it forms spores and reproduces like a mushroom. It seems to be a single individual, yet, if broken into pieces, each individual piece not only can live indefinitely by itself, but can also, if it meets its better or worser half again, merge with it to become again one individual!

Until last night I had never seen another paradox— the flying squirrel. Many other country dwellers, I imagine, have also never seen one, for, though they are said to inhabit forested regions throughout all America, they are so exclusively nocturnal that one may live surrounded by them without ever knowing that they exist. It was one of my cats who brought me a specimen last night, and who made an unusual fuss over it, almost as though he knew that it was a novelty which I should examine. My first impulse was, as usual, to scold. But he had only done what most naturalists who profess, as he does not, to love nature would have done when meeting a strange animal for the first time. There are only two differences. One is that whereas the cat "kills," the naturalist "collects." The other is that the naturalist would have stuffed the squirrel and that the cat stuffed himself. His belly, I am afraid, is a museum which has in its time housed a great variety of specimens.

Some modern painters have, of course, gone to living nature in their search for formal design. Georgia O'Keefe's often scandalous analogies are, in America at least, especially well known. But it surprises me that most of the abstractionists who go in for the geometrical seem to prefer as a source of inspiration the man-made machine, rather than the plant which was the original inventor of most geometrical design. Such design hardly exists in inanimate nature, except in the case of the misleading crystal, which so often looks as though it were the product of organic growth and seems to mock the creations of that life in which it has never had any share. But living things are almost always "well-designed."

Most of the functionless pseudo-machines which one kind of abstractionist designs on canvas or realizes in metal masses, or the still more grotesque "mobiles" of the avant-garde galleries, strike me as comically futile. They are not nearly so beautiful as the actual and purposeful steam turbines, electric generators, and gantry cranes which they seem to be attempting to improve upon. And however philistine my reaction may be, they generally suggest to me not their often beautiful originals, but those insane mechanical fantasies which Mr. Goldberg once made famous.

If I were a painter or a sculptor more interested in design than in story-telling, it seems to me that I should go instead to the living organisms, which, to anyone who looks closely, exhibit many examples of "modern" geometrical design. I should go to the blossom, which usually builds up a pattern of fives or threes; to the seed pods, which come in an infinite variety of boxes, flasks, and urns; even, if I wanted a "mobile," to the ripe fruit of the wild geranium, whose effective catapult was tossing hard round seeds many millenniums before the military engineers of the Renaissance discovered that the same principle could be used to hurl boulders at an enemy. Curiously enough, it seems that the smaller the living unit, the more exquisitely elaborate and perfect the form will be. Pollen grains which no man saw before the invention of the microscope come in an endless variety of regular shapes, and many of them are embossed or engraved with patterns which rival in intricacy those sculptured on the glass shells of the microscopic bivalves called diatoms.

Man is a lonely creature. A very great deal—perhaps all—of his religion and his art has been an attempt to discover or to read into the universe outside himself something which corresponds to certain things which he finds *in* himself. So far as literature is concerned that means finding, especially, purposes and values. So far as the plastic arts are concerned it means finding regular design—for geometry is hardly less important to man than morality is.

In his pictures he schematizes landscapes or arranges groups of figures into pyramidal or other patterns because it comforts him to sense such patterns in a representation of nature, and he arranges the trees and the hills of his landscapes into similar patterns. But the formalists who conclude therefore that the purest art is that which gives us design itself, rather than design discovered in or imposed upon recognizable objects, are quite wrong. And they are quite wrong because it is not the mere existence of the design, but the discovery (or the illusion) that it exists in nature, in something outside ourselves, which reassures us.

In nature itself, it is not the grand aggregation of growing things, but the individual plant or part of a plant, which unmistakably reveals that the design is actually there, that nature herself can geometrize. Perhaps no more than the first faint beginnings of what the philospher or the poet will recognize as purpose or the establishment of values can be found there, but humanly recognizable design is already fully developed. One might travel to all the famous "beauty spots" of the earth and come home again uncomforted—not sure, I mean, that even formal design as we recognize it exists outside ourselves. But almost any roadside weed, closely looked at, will demonstrate beyond any possible doubt that it does. We are not alone in understanding or needing it.

Perhaps an unwillingness to acknowledge that fact is the perverse reason that leads so many modern artists to prefer to find form in machinery. If I am right in a certain suspicion which has forced itself upon me, our tendency to get away from nature is an expression of a fundamental perversity which is leading man to prefer a sense of isolation, to stress rather than to minimize his uniqueness and his aloneness. He seems increasingly to prefer to believe that he is not part of nature but something separate from it, and therefore to be most pleased when the world in which he lives is as completely as possible artificial. Even his pictures must be pictures, not of natural objects, but either of states of soul or of the machine. God made the country and man made the town. Man belongs, ergo, with brick, and mortar, and iron.

Personally, I feel both happier and more secure when I am reminded that I have the backing of something older and perhaps more permanent than I am—the something, I mean, which taught the flower to count five and the beetle to know that spots are more pleasing if arranged in a definite order. Some of the most important secrets are, they assure me, known to others besides myself.

CHAPTER 10

MAKING THE DAYS
SEEM LONG

This morning I saw through my window the first idle flakes of the year's first real snow. Small, scattered, and casual, they might have passed almost unnoticed. But it is thus that great things begin, and to a practiced eye they had the air of meaning business.

They were not fluffy like the playful flakes of a precocious flurry, nor wet like the end-of-the-season falls, which turn first to sleet and then to rain. Instead, they were the single, hard, sparkling little crystals which look as though they intended to remain just that, and come down with quiet confidence, as though they knew they are merely the advance guard of many to follow and to support them. The first tender green of April is not more deceptively tentative, more unspectacular in appearance. Neither is it surer of itself. Equally, the first green and the first white seem to say, "I know that my time has come. It is now that I shall inherit the earth."

Such things as this one never quite remembers. One recognizes them when they appear again, as one recognizes the opening bars of a symphony one could not whistle or hum. What is to follow is not so much re-called as prepared for, and it will magically combine the charm of the familiar with the charm of the new. Memory can never reconstruct for itself the infinite, felicitous detail. Winter, like spring and like Mozart, is always richer and more varied than one remembered it.

I have, when I care to look back at them, my charts and my tables. On the graph of the daily maxima and minima recorded by my thermometer, the coming of winter means two irregular lines which erratically rise and fall while they tend ever downward. In my diary it means, less nakedly, a series of visible phenomena, from the blazing of the dying leaves to the hardening of the ground and the gradual fading of color, until blackness and whiteness come to dominate. But no sum of such details will add up to any adequate account of what has been happening. It fails, as any analysis of any work of art must fail, to suggest the mighty, interrelated whole-ness of a process whose inevitable logic is its greatest secret.

Any analogy with winter dooms us to choose a lesser thing for comparison with that which we intend to exalt. What is now about to begin Thoreau grandly denominated "that grand old poem called Winter." One is not likely to better him when he is, as here, at his best. And yet even a poem is not really so complex a thing as this winter which operates not only upon the mind, but upon all the senses as well, and which one does not merely contemplate because one is also a part of it. Perhaps it is a poem more nearly than it is anything else. But it is also a drama, a symphony, and a picture.

Some small part of the drama is visible even from a box seat in front of a window through which one may catch glimpses of birds and beasts whose existence is affected far more drastically than ours, and one may guess also at what is going on below the surface of the snow; below even the surface of soil, where innumerable creatures are sleeping—almost as deeply as the very tree roots—a sleep from which some will awaken, but which, for some others, will pass into imperceptible death. That same window may become also a picture frame, though it is the frame of a picture which changes as no painted picture can, a picture which passes through a series of modulations, each in itself as beautiful as though it were a final end—to become successively the picture of summer, the picture of autumn, and finally the picture of winter.

The very style of the artist seems to change, as he gives his allegiance to one school after another. In sum-

mer he was all for Dutch or German minuteness. He
cluttered his canvas with detail; affected on a perhaps
unsuitably large scale the methods of the miniaturist.
As autumn came, he began to simplify, to go in for
broader, bolder effects, and then, as the snow came, he
realized the impressiveness of large areas and large
masses. At last, when everything except the largest fea-
tures of any landscape has been buried, he becomes almost an abstractionist. There seems nothing left to paint
except an idea.

But one is not compelled to remain always standing
before the picture frame, or confined to the spectator's
side of the proscenium. One may walk into the picture,
become part of the poem, or even participate in the
drama itself. From no mere canvas does the wind actually blow; there is no poem from which a snowflake
can detach itself to melt upon the cheek. From every
man-made poem, or picture, or drama, one is to some
extent excluded. A certain separateness from it is necessary if it is to be art at all. We must contemplate and
we must not intervene. But of nature's poems and pictures we are invited to become a part. This winter which
is just coming in offers the detachment of an aesthetic
experience, combined with the immediacy of living.

I know now that my judgment of this morning's in-
tentions was correct. The tentative fall did grow steadily
more confident and purposeful; incredibly, the sum of
the almost infinitesimal, laid gently down upon another

infinitesimal, added up to a palpable thickness. Within a few hours the snowplow was making its first trip up my road, and within a few hours more that road had become impassable again.

In our well-organized and dependably functioning society, the threat implied is remote. I know that our responsible First Selectman will employ the machines at his disposal to re-establish my access to the village upon which I am dependent. It is only rarely that I am cut off for more than a few hours even from the train which would take me to the city, should I want to go there. The possibility of being seriously snowbound is hardly more than theoretical. And yet, ready as a whole organization is to see that I do not even need to be rescued, I have a sense I could never have had in the city itself, of what the threat of winter might be. And we are so curiously constituted that terrors of which only a shadow remains become strangely exhilarating. They transform themselves into their aesthetic counterparts, and become almost like those provided by melodrama, or even by tragedy. The danger has disappeared, but the adventure is left.

Perhaps to enjoy the aesthetic pleasure of even a simulated threat without a twinge of remembered terror, one needs to be among the fortunate who have never had to struggle too frequently in the past with the real thing. Vilhjalmur Stefansson remarks that for such an adventure as an Arctic expedition, people who have led a hard life are no good. Your common sailor, your eskimo even, grows sullenly rebellious when asked to meet conditions only a little more rigorous than those which are his common lot. Though his food has never been good, it is tremendously important to him that it should not be even a little bit worse, and since danger is his business, he runs no unnecessary risks. For an adventure one must have adventurers, and that means usually the privileged—say, a college youth who has enjoyed all the "privileges" of his class. He may find a real pleasure in being compelled to eat what the sailor would rebel against, and will voluntarily face a danger for the sake of some intangible achievement. He can, in other words, savor the thing aesthetically, and an adventure is merely a hardship aesthetically considered.

I have observed the two attitudes traceable to two similar pasts in the case of my two cats. One of them was raised by an unusually devoted mother in a human environment where he never met anything but kindness. Before he opened his eyes, he was conditioned to assume that whatever he needed would be provided, and that his comfort, his convenience even, would be considered by his human protectors before their own. The other was born under a farmyard porch in the depth of winter, and grew up precariously in a rough world of dogs, of children, and of adults who barely tolerated him.

According to one theory of education the first should be "spoiled" and the second prepared to meet the world.

Yet when the snow comes, the one who should be a softie takes it as a delightful adventure. He races here and there, and delightedly runs into the drifts after snow balls. The other, who ought to be tough, is merely distressed, and when I coax him out of doors he sits howling dismally on the doorstep until admitted again.

One attitude is precisely that of the sportsman, the other that of those to whom what is called adventure is no more than hardship. Contemplating the two has compelled me to revise my opinion concerning one of the principles of modern education. The theory that children should be made to feel absolutely secure and perpetually surrounded by love used to strike me as dubious. It would give them, it seemed to me, a very false idea of what the world is like, would prepare them very badly for the shock of discovering that love cannot be taken for granted and that environments are not always propitious. But perhaps perfect security at the right time makes for boldness in the future, and perhaps to meet distress too early is to be made forever timid.

I must add, nevertheless, that the adventurous cat is also and in other ways unmistakably the extrovert, and I am not one of those who assume that any personality, even tempered by introversion, is to just that extent unfortunate and undesirable. Of the two cats it is the unadventurous one who is conspicuously fond of music —and of the very best music too. But that is another story.

In my own small domain, for which the state takes no responsibility, the change is more drastic than on the roads. Up until now I strolled casually out the door to the garage or the poultry house. Now even a trip to the bird-feeder to replenish its store takes on the character of an expedition, which must be prepared for in a special costume. Creatures more exposed than I must change more drastically their habits. Hardly had the snow begun before the birds, seeming to sense what was impending, began to come in greater and greater numbers to feed. The woodpeckers hammered persistently at the suet; the chickadees cued up, waiting their turn to get at the peanut butter—become the favorite food of these creatures brought within the grocery stores' sphere of influence. Even the wary jays, ordinarily disinclined to approach after the human inhabitants of the house are stirring, came in great flocks to snatch and carry away large morsels of food, each sufficient to make several meals for a smaller bird.

On previous occasions the snow had also precipitated more violent dramas. Once it had been responsible for the disappearance of the ducks whose pond my frogs later inherited. A trail of bloody feathers beside footprints in the snow told the tale of a marauding fox. All fall the ducks had been equally accessible, but the killer had smaller game to be caught in regions more remote from the danger of man. Now winter had made him bold. He must indeed have dared to come in daylight, for the door was closed against him at night.

Shut snugly indoors, as at this moment I am, these dramas seem rather remote. Somewhat shamefacedly, I confess that it is thus most of my wintertime is passed, and that for me a little struggle with the elements— necessary as it is—goes a rather long way. The coming in again is likely to be the best part of any expedition, and the sense of peace and remoteness the best part of the season. It is good to discover how self-sufficient one can be, and perhaps with this sense of reserved well-being there is mingled just a little of the Lucretian complacency—the pleasure of realizing, not that others must struggle, but merely that I need not.

Even a definitely closed road, especially a road just difficult enough to discourage travel, is not an unmixed evil. Nearly everyone goes too many places too frequently, and snow can be a great alleviator of the American restlessness. If I cannot get out to the world, the world also cannot get in to me, and there are times when that fact seems good, no matter which way one looks at it. Overly gregarious people sometimes pity me for being cut off, but there are days, weeks even, when I see nothing funny in the old story of the London *Times* and the headline with which it announced a storm over the Channel: "CONTINENT ISO-LATED." I do not expect the world to miss me, but if anyone feels cut off, it is not I.

Hamlet boasted that he could be confined in a nut-shell and feel himself lord of infinite space. I shall certainly not go so far as that. I know what claustrophobia is like, and the roomiest nutshell would not be enough. This may be what Hamlet meant by his bad dreams. But I can sometimes be glad that for a few days at least I am not forced—or even tempted—to go further than my own legs will carry me. "Water," Samuel Johnson once said in rebuke to Boswell, who was about to launch into a comparison between the Bay of Naples and a Scottish harbor, "looks much the same everywhere." That has generally been cited to prove Johnson had no appreciation of natural scenery. And perhaps he did not. But his remark might be taken to mean just what Thoreau's boast that he had traveled extensively in Concord certainly did mean—namely, that nature is always beautiful, and that there is less danger of exhausting one's own few acres than there is of traveling so widely that one never really sees anything. Snow, like water, "looks much the same everywhere." But it is very much worth looking at, nevertheless, wherever one may find it. I have walked through the white drifts near the summit of the Jungfrau in July, and I am glad that I have—partly because I now know that, beautiful as it was there, it is hardly less so in Connecticut, where I can observe it more at my leisure and get to know it better.

Your Hindu fakir sits on nails in the public square and meditates on eternity. To be able to do so is perhaps to offer proof of a detachment achieved through an admirable discipline. Weak westerners like myself need, however, aids to contemplation rather than opportunities to demonstrate over what obstacles we can triumph, and a little winter isolation provides a very favorable set of circumstances. In rare moments, it will bring one as close as one's individual nature makes possible to the mystic's sense of oneness, but on a more rational level it makes possible also a special kind of detachment, and it forces one to face up to conclusions from which distraction would furnish an escape. New thoughts cannot be expected too frequently, but it is something to find oneself, in Mr. Frost's now famous phrase, "More sure of all I thought was true."

I know that not everyone likes to be alone, even for a short time. What surprises me, however, is the fact that those who do not, are so often the very ones who say that they are very happy and that they love to live. How, I often wonder, can they possibly know. When are they quiet enough to ask the question or to get the answer? So much of life passes in busy unconsciousness. Most of the time that most men are either working or playing, they are too "occupied" to be aware even that they are living. Someone else, so it always seems to me, might just as well be doing these things for them. They gather in groups as though each felt the need to have others assure him that he really exists. Why, I wonder, does he not shut himself up somewhere for a day and find out? If the answer should turn out to be in the negative, then he might at least reconcile himself to the fact; if in the affirmative, then he might have the question happily settled once and for all. He would not have to go through life as though afraid of learning its answer.

Those who talk frankly of their need for "distraction" are sometimes frowned upon by the serious minded, but those who boast that they want always to be "occupied" are usually admired. And yet the two things turn out very often to be the same thing, or at least to have the same object, and I have no more respect for the man who must always be busy than for the one who must always be distracted. We are even advised to take our minds off ourselves, but it seems to me—whatever the psychiatrists may say about the minority who pass through their hands—that a far larger number of people should be advised, once at least, to put their minds *on* themselves, where, obviously, they have not very often been. "We only live once" is a saying most inappropriate on the lips where it is most often found, for they most commonly are the lips of those who seem determined to be unaware that they are living that once.

Sometimes a sympathetic acquaintance who knows what I have been doing—and what I have not been doing—asks me pityingly if "the days do not seem long?" Of course they do. That is one of the best things about them. How else, in heaven's name, should one want them to seem? What confession—if one pretends to find existence sweet—could be more dreadful than speaking happily of the time which seems short; than to say, not with regret, but with an air of self-

congratulation, "I do not know where the day went"—
or the week, or the month, or the year, or, finally, the
lifetime itself. I have often been bored at the cocktail
or the dinner party, and boredom can be a dreadful
thing—while it is going on. But it is curiously difficult
to remember. It usually leaves no scar, and I am not
sure that I always resent the hours of boredom as much
as I do the time spent when I was merely distracted.
When one is bored, one at least knows that one is alive,
and life is lengthened, unpleasantly though it may be.

But the day which is delightfully long when meas-
ured in terms of that psychological time which alone
means anything, is more often than not spent in one's
own home and its immediate familiar environs; the day
when one goes nowhere, has no engagements, and when
the only companion is someone known well enough and
long enough to be almost another self. Those are the
days which "seem long" and would be welcome to seem
even longer. Not one moment passes unnoticed, not one
fails to make its contribution. If all one's days counted
for so much, then three score years and ten would not
be a short time. And if one cannot live such days without being aware that time is passing, no matter how
slowly, if every tick of the clock is recognized as count-
ing off one more half-second deducted from those al-
lotted, that fact grows out of one of the ineluctable
contingencies of our life, for we cannot remember that
we are living without remembering also that time is
passing.

Last night the temperature dropped to below zero for
the first time this season. Today the air is still and the
sunshine sparkling, but there is an additional bite in the
air which gives another reason for coming in out of it
quickly, and for spending most of the day in the house.
Even there, where it is as warm as one could wish, the
fur of the cats crackles when one strokes it, as though it
had maintained some kind of sympathy with the out-of-
doors. This, I can see now, will be one of those days I
have been attempting to describe. It is possible that I
may have some thought I never had before, that I shall
see something in a new light. But nothing of the sort is
necessary to make life worth living. The old will do
very nicely—the old thoughts and the old delights—
for they will not seem old to me. The next sixteen
hours will be priceless, and before I go to bed I shall
be able to say:

> Be fair or foul, come rain or shine
> The joys I have possessed in spite of fate are mine;
> Not Heaven itself upon the past has power
> What has been, has been, and I have had my hour.

That, I submit, is what ought to be called "success
in life."

CHAPTER 11

THE COLLOID AND
THE CRYSTAL

That first real snow inadequately celebrated in the preceding chapter was soon followed by a second. Over the radio the weatherman talked lengthily about cold masses and warm masses, about what was moving out to sea and what wasn't. Did Benjamin Franklin, I wondered, know what he was starting when it first occurred to him to trace by correspondence the course of storms? From my stationary position the most reasonable explanation seemed to be simply that winter had not quite liked the looks of the landscape as she first made it up. She was changing her sheets.

Another forty-eight hours brought one of those nights ideal for frosting the panes. When I came down to breakfast, two of the windows were almost opaque and the others were etched with graceful, fernlike sprays of ice which looked rather like the impressions left in rocks by some of the antediluvian plants, and they were almost as beautiful as anything which the living can achieve. Nothing else which has never lived looks so much as though it were actually informed with life.

I resisted, I am proud to say, the almost universal impulse to scratch my initials into one of the surfaces. The effect, I knew, would not be an improvement. But so, of course, do those less virtuous than I. That indeed is precisely why they scratch. The impulse to mar and to destroy is as ancient and almost as nearly universal as the impulse to create. The one is an easier way than the other of demonstrating power. Why else should anyone not hungry prefer a dead rabbit to a live one? Not even those horrible Dutch painters of bloody still—or shall we say stilled?—lifes can have really believed that their subjects were more beautiful dead.

Indoors it so happened that a Christmas cactus had chosen this moment to bloom. Its lush blossoms, fuchsia-shaped but pure red rather than magenta, hung at the drooping ends of strange, thick stems and outlined themselves in blood against the glistening background of the frosty pane—jungle flower against frost-flower; the warm beauty that breathes and lives and dies competing with the cold beauty that burgeons, not because it wants to, but merely because it is obeying the laws of physics which require that crystals shall take the shape they have always taken since the world began. The effect of red flower against white tracery was almost too theatrical, not quite in good taste perhaps. My eye recoiled in shock and sought through a clear area of the glass the more normal out-of-doors.

On the snow-capped summit of my bird-feeder a chickadee pecked at the new-fallen snow and swallowed a few of the flakes which serve him in lieu of the water he sometimes sadly lacks when there is nothing except ice too solid to be picked at. A downy woodpecker was hammering at a lump of suet and at the coconut full of peanut butter. One nuthatch was dining while the mate waited his—or was it her?—turn. The woodpecker announces the fact that he is a male by the bright red spot on the back of his neck, but to me, at least, the sexes of the nuthatch are indistinguishable. I shall never know whether it is the male or the female who eats first. And that is a pity. If I knew, I could say, like the Ugly Duchess, "and the moral of that is . . ."

But I soon realized that at the moment the frosted windows were what interested me most—especially the fact that there is no other natural phenomenon in which the lifeless mocks so closely the living. One might almost think that the frostflower had got the idea from the leaf and the branch if one did not know how inconceivably more ancient the first is. No wonder that enthusiastic biologists in the nineteenth century, anxious to conclude that there was no qualitative difference between life and chemical processes, tried to believe that the crystal furnished the link, that its growth was actually the same as the growth of a living organism. But excusable though the fancy was, no one, I think, believes anything of the sort today. Protoplasm is a colloid and the colloids are fundamentally different from the crystalline substances. Instead of crystallizing they jell, and life in its simplest known form is a shapeless blob of rebellious jelly rather than a crystal eternally obeying the most ancient law.

No man ever saw a dinosaur. The last of these giant reptiles was dead eons before the most dubious half-man surveyed the world about him. Not even the dinosaurs ever cast their dim eyes upon many of the still earlier creatures which preceded them. Life changes so rapidly that its later phases know nothing of those which preceded them. But the frostflower is older than the dinosaur, older than the protozoan, older no doubt than the enzyme or the ferment. Yet it is precisely what it has always been. Millions of years before there were any eyes to see it, millions of years before any life existed, it grew in its own special way, crystallized along its preordained lines of cleavage, stretched out its pseudo-branches and pseudo-leaves. It was beautiful before beauty itself existed.

We find it difficult to conceive a world except in

terms of purpose, of will, or of intention. At the thought of the something without beginning and presumably without end, of something which is, nevertheless, regular though blind, and organized without any end in view, the mind reels. Constituted as we are it is easier to conceive how the slime floating upon the waters might become in time Homo sapiens than it is to imagine how so complex a thing as a crystal could have always been and can always remain just what it is— complicated and perfect but without any meaning, even for itself. How can the lifeless even obey a law?

To a mathematical physicist I once confessed somewhat shamefacedly that I had never been able to understand how inanimate nature managed to follow so invariably and so promptly her own laws. If I flip a coin across a table, it will come to rest at a certain point. But before it stops at just that point, many factors must be taken into consideration. There is the question of the strength of the initial impulse, of the exact amount of resistance offered by the friction of that particular table top, and of the density of the air at the moment. It would take a physicist a long time to work out the problem and he could achieve only an approximation at that. Yet presumably the coin will stop exactly where it should. Some very rapid calculations have to be made before it can do so, and they are, presumably, always accurate.

And then, just as I was blushing at what I supposed he must regard as my folly, the mathematician came to

my rescue by informing me that Laplace had been puzzled by exactly the same fact. "Nature laughs at the
difficulties of integration," he remarked—and by "integration" he meant, of course, the mathematician's word
for the process involved when a man solves one of
the differential equations to which he has reduced the
laws of motion.

When my Christmas cactus blooms so theatrically a
few inches in front of the frost-covered pane, it also is
obeying laws but obeying them much less rigidly and in
a different way. It blooms at about Christmastime because it has got into the habit of doing so, because, one
is tempted to say, it wants to. As a matter of fact it was,
this year, not a Christmas cactus but a New Year's cactus, and because of this unpredictability I would like to
call it "he," not "it." His flowers assume their accustomed shape and take on their accustomed color. But
not as the frostflowers follow their predestined pattern. Like me, the cactus has a history which stretches
back over a long past full of changes and developments.
He has not always been merely obeying fixed laws. He
has resisted and rebelled; he has attempted novelties,
passed through many phases. Like all living things he
has had a will of his own. He has made laws, not
merely obeyed them.

"Life," so the platitudinarian is fond of saying, "is
strange." But from our standpoint it is not really so
strange as those things which have no life and yet
nevertheless move in their predestined orbits and "act"

though they do not "behave." At the very least one ought to say that if life is strange there is nothing about it more strange than the fact that it has its being in a universe so astonishingly shared on the one hand by "things" and on the other by "creatures," that man himself is both a "thing" which obeys the laws of chemistry or physics and a "creature" who to some extent defies them. No other contrast, certainly not the contrast between the human being and the animal, or the animal and the plant, or even the spirit and the body, is so tremendous as this contrast between what lives and what does not.

To think of the lifeless as merely inert, to make the contrast merely in terms of a negative, is to miss the real strangeness. Not the shapeless stone which seems to be merely waiting to be acted upon but the snowflake or the frostflower is the true representative of the lifeless universe as opposed to ours. They represent plainly, as the stone does not, the fixed and perfect system of organization which includes the sun and its planets, includes therefore this earth itself, but against which life has set up its seemingly puny opposition. Order and obedience are the primary characteristics of that which is not alive. The snowflake eternally obeys its one and only law: "Be thou six pointed"; the planets their one and only: "Travel thou in an ellipse." The astronomer can tell where the North Star will be ten thousand years hence; the botanist cannot tell where the dandelion will bloom tomorrow.

Life is rebellious and anarchial, always testing the supposed immutability of the rules which the nonliving changelessly accepts. Because the snowflake goes on doing as it was told, its story up to the end of time was finished when it first assumed the form which it has kept ever since. But the story of every living thing is still in the telling. It may hope and it may try. Moreover, though it may succeed or fail, it will certainly change. No form of frostflower ever became extinct. Such, if you like, is its glory. But such also is the fact which makes it alien. It may melt but it cannot die.

If I wanted to contemplate what is to me the deepest of all mysteries, I should choose as my object lesson a snowflake under a lens and an amoeba under the microscope. To a detached observer—if one can possibly imagine any observer who *could* be detached when faced with such an ultimate choice—the snowflake would certainly seem the "higher" of the two. Against its intricate glistening perfection one would have to place a shapeless, slightly turbid glob, perpetually oozing out in this direction or that but not suggesting so strongly as the snowflake does, intelligence and plan. Crystal and colloid, the chemist would call them, but what an inconceivable contrast those neutral terms imply! Like the star, the snowflake seems to declare the glory of God, while the promise of the amoeba, given only perhaps to itself, seems only contemptible. But its jelly holds, nevertheless, not only its promise but ours also, while the snowflake represents some achievement which we cannot possibly share. After the passage of billions of years, one can see and be aware of the other, but the relationship can never be reciprocal. Even after these billions of years no aggregate of colloids can be as beautiful as the crystal always was, but it can know, as the crystal cannot, what beauty is.

Even to admire too much or too exclusively the alien kind of beauty is dangerous. Much as I love and am moved by the grand, inanimate forms of nature, I am always shocked and a little frightened by those of her professed lovers to whom landscape is the most important thing, and to whom landscape is merely a matter of forms and colors. If they see or are moved by an animal or flower, it is to them merely a matter of a picturesque completion and their fellow creatures are no more than decorative details. But without some continuous awareness of the two great realms of the inanimate and the animate there can be no love of nature as I understand it, and what is worse, there must be a sort of disloyalty to our cause, to us who are colloid, not crystal. The pantheist who feels the oneness of all living things, I can understand; perhaps indeed he and I are in essential agreement. But the ultimate All is not one thing, but two. And because the alien half is in its way as proud and confident and successful as our half, its fundamental difference may not be disregarded with impunity. Of us and all we stand for, the enemy is not so much death as the not-living, or rather that great sys-

tem which succeeds without ever having had the need
to be alive. The frostflower is not merely a wonder; it
is also a threat and a warning. How admirable, it seems
to say, not living can be! What triumphs mere immutable law can achieve!

Some of Charles Pierce's strange speculations about
the possibility that "natural law" is not law at all but
merely a set of habits fixed more firmly than any habits we know anything about in ourselves or in the animals suggest the possibility that the snowflake was not,
after all, always inanimate, that it merely surrendered
at some time impossibly remote the life which once
achieved its perfect organization. Yet even if we can imagine such a thing to be true, it serves only to warn us
all the more strongly against the possibility that what
we call the living might in the end succumb also to the
seduction of the immutably fixed.

No student of the anthill has ever failed to be astonished either into admiration or horror by what is
sometimes called the perfection of its society. Though
even the anthill can change its ways, though even ant
individuals—ridiculous as the conjunction of the two
words may seem—can sometimes make choices, the perfection of the techniques, the regularity of the habits
almost suggest the possibility that the insect is on its
way back to inanition, that, vast as the difference still is,
an anthill crystallizes somewhat as a snowflake does. But
not even the anthill, nothing else indeed in the whole

known universe is so perfectly planned as one of these same snowflakes. Would, then, the ultimately planned society be, like the anthill, one in which no one makes plans, any more than a snowflake does? From the cradle in which it is not really born to the grave where it is only a little deader than it always was, the ant-citizen follows a plan to the making of which he no longer contributes anything.

Perhaps we men represent the ultimate to which the rebellion, begun so long ago in some amoeba-like jelly, can go. And perhaps the inanimate is beginning the slow process of subduing us again. Certainly the psychologist and the philosopher are tending more and more to think of us as creatures who obey laws rather than as creatures of will and responsibility. We are, they say, "conditioned" by this or by that. Even the greatest heroes are studied on the assumption that they can be "accounted for" by something outside themselves. They are, it is explained, "the product of forces." All the emphasis is placed, not upon that power to resist and rebel which we were once supposed to have, but upon the "influences" which "formed us." Men are made by society, not society by men. History as well as character "obeys laws." In their view, we crystallize in obedience to some dictate from without instead of moving in conformity with something within.

And so my eye goes questioningly back to the frosted pane. While I slept the graceful pseudo-fronds crept across the glass, assuming, as life itself does, an intricate organization. "Why live," they seem to say, "when we can be beautiful, complicated, and orderly without the uncertainty and effort required of a living thing? Once we were all that was. Perhaps some day we shall be all that is. Why not join us?"

Last summer no clod or no stone would have been heard if it had asked such a question. The hundreds of things which walked and sang, the millions which crawled and twined were all having their day. What was dead seemed to exist only in order that the living might live upon it. The plants were busy turning the inorganic into green life and the animals were busy turning that green into red. When we moved, we walked mostly upon grass. Our pre-eminence was unchallenged.

On this winter day nothing seems so successful as the frostflower. It thrives on the very thing which has driven some of us indoors or underground and which has been fatal to many. It is having now its hour of triumph, as we before had ours. Like the cactus flower itself, I am a hothouse plant. Even my cats gaze dreamily out of the window at a universe which is no longer theirs.

How are we to resist, if resist we can? This house into which I have withdrawn is merely an expedient and it serves only my mere physical existence. What mental or spiritual convictions, what will to maintain to my own kind of existence can I assert? For me it is not

enough merely to say, as I do say, that I shall resist
the invitation to submerge myself into a crystalline society and to stop planning in order that I may be
planned for. Neither is it enough to go further, as I do
go, and to insist that the most important thing about a
man is not that part of him which is "the product of
forces" but that part, however small it may be, which
enables him to become something other than what the
most accomplished sociologist, working in conjunction
with the most accomplished psychologist, could predict
that he would be.

I need, so I am told, a faith, something outside myself to which I can be loyal. And with that I agree, in
my own way. I am on what I call "our side," and I
know, though vaguely, what I think that is. Wordsworth's God had his dwelling in the light of setting
suns. But the God who dwells there seems to me most
probably the God of the atom, the star, and the crystal.
Mine, if I have one, reveals Himself in another class of
phenomena. He makes the grass green and the blood
red.

CHAPTER 12

POSTSCRIPT

More than twenty-five years ago I first bought a house in the country. My motives were various, but as in the case of many another man who acquires something he never had before, the most compelling was the fact that my wife wanted it. Among the reasons I gave myself to explain my acquiescence, the possibility that I might some day be writing about nature was certainly not one. As a matter of fact I had been leading a double life, in the city and out of it, for almost a quarter of a century before it occurred to me. Then one evening when I was reading with delight about someone else's feeling for his countryside, I said to myself that it would be nice if I could do it too.

Until then I had never realized what had been happening to me. I still thought that I thought the country was a place where one went to get away from the fatigues of the city. Its virtues were still supposed to be largely negative and I had never realized how, in actual fact, I had long been regarding it as the principal scene of those activities for the sake of which I made a living elsewhere, how completely it had become the place where it seemed to me that I must live or have no being. Since then I have seen myself referred to somewhat condescendingly as a "nature writer," and though I did not mind it a bit, I was set to wondering just what a nature writer might be and just why or from just what he should be distinguished by his special label.

A great many people, I am afraid, do not even care to know. When they hear the phrase they think of "the birds and the bees"—a useful device in the sex education of children but hardly, they think, an occupation for a grown man. A biologist is all right and so is a sportsman. But a nature writer can hardly expect more than a shrug from the realistic or the robust.

The more literary quote Wordsworth: "Nature never did betray the heart that loved her" or "to me the meanest flower that blows can give thoughts that do often lie too deep for tears." But Darwin, they say, exploded such ideas nearly a century ago. Even Tennyson knew better: "Nature red in tooth and claw." We can't very well learn anything from all that. Ours are desperate times. The only hope for today lies in the study of politics, sociology, and economics. If a nature writer is someone who advocates a return to nature then he must be a sentimentalist and a very old-fashioned one at that.

But why, then, should I have discovered that my week ends and my summers in the country were becoming more and more important, that I spent more and more time looking at and thinking about plants and animals and birds, that I began to feel the necessity of writing about what I had seen and thought? Why, finally, when I saw fifteen free months ahead of me, should I have been sure that I wanted to go back to the southwestern desert to see what an entirely different, only half-known natural environment might have to say to me?

It was more than a mere casual interest in natural history as a hobby. Certainly it was also more than the mere fact that the out-of-doors is healthful and relaxing. I was not merely being soothed and refreshed by an escape from the pressures of urban life. I was seeking for something, and I got at least the conviction that there was something I really was learning. I seemed to be getting a glimpse of some wisdom of which I had less than an inkling before.

Actually, of course, nature writing does flourish quite vigorously today as a separate department of literature even though it does remain to some extent a thing apart, addressed chiefly to a group of readers called "nature lovers" who are frequently referred to by outsiders in the same condescending tone they would use in speaking of prohibitionists, diet cranks, Holy Rollers, or the followers—if there still are any—of the late Mr. Coué. And that makes me sometimes wonder whether its very importance as a "department of literature" does not mean that what was once an almost inevitable motive in most imaginative writing has become something recognizably special, for the reason that most writers of novels and poems and plays no longer find the contemplation of nature relevant to their purposes—at least to the same extent they once did. And I wonder also whether that seeming fact is merely the result of urban living, or whether "merely" is not the wrong term to use in reference to a phenomenon which may mean a great deal more than the mere disappearance from fiction of apostrophes to the mountains.

A generation ago the first page of the epoch-making *Cambridge History of English Literature* listed among the enduring characteristics of the English people, "love of nature." That phrase covers something which has meant a good many different things at different times. But would it have suggested itself to a critic who was concerned only with the most esteemed English or American books of our time? Is there any love of nature—as distinguished from an intellectual approval of the processes of biology—in Bernard Shaw? Does T. S. Eliot find much gladness in contemplating nature? Does Joyce's apostrophe to a river count, and is Hemingway's enthusiasm for the slaughter of animals really to be considered as a modern expression of even that devotion to blood sports which, undoubtedly, really is a rather incongruous aspect of the Anglo-Saxon race's love of nature? In America Robert Frost is almost the only poet whose work is universally recognized as of major importance and in which the loving contemplation of natural phenomena seems a central activity from which the poetry springs.

All this is probably the result of something more than mere fashion. True, ridicule of conventional description in fiction is no new thing, and Mark Twain once tested his theory that readers always skip it by inserting a paragraph which told how a solitary esophagus might have been seen winging its way across the sky. It is true also that observations of natural phenomena do still sometimes get into fiction. *The Grapes of Wrath* begins with the symbolic use of a turtle crossing a highway and nearly everybody knows that at least one tree did grow in Brooklyn. But somewhere along the road they have traveled, most moderns have lost the sense that nature is the most significant background of human life. They see their characters as part of society or, more specifically, members of some profession or slaves at some industry, rather than as part of nature. Neither her appearances nor her ways any longer seem—to use a favorite modern term—as "relevant" as they once did. She is not often, nowadays, invoked to furnish the resolution of an emotional problem.

Whistler was probably the first English-speaking writer ever to say flatly "Nature is wrong." Of course he meant to be shocking and he also meant "artistically wrong"—unpictorial or badly composed. And goodness only knows most contemporary painting is the product of hearty agreement with this dictum. Either natural objects are so distorted in the effort to correct nature's wrongness that they are just barely recognizable, or the artist, refusing to look at nature at all, plays at being God by attempting to create a whole new universe of man-made shapes. In either case the assumption is that modern man is more at home and gets more emotional satisfaction in this world of his own making than in the world which nature gave him.

Only the most extreme forms of the most desperately "experimental" writing go anything like so far. Only the poets of the Dada produce literary analogies of abstract painting. But without being, for the most part, even aware of a theory about what they are doing, many novelists and poets have obviously ceased to feel that the significant physical setting for their characters or sentiments is the fields or woods, or that the intellectual and emotional context of their difficulties and problems is the natural world rather than that of exclusively human concepts. This amounts to a good deal more than a mere loss of faith in the dogma that nature never did betray the heart that loved her. It also amounts to a good deal more than the somewhat romantic Victorian distress in the face of her red tooth and red claw. It means that the writer finds neither God dwelling in the light of setting suns nor a very significant aspect of the problem of evil in nature's often careless cruelty. Faced with either her beauty or her ruthlessness, his reaction is more likely to be only, "so what?" Man's own achievements, follies, and crimes seem to him to lie in a different realm.

As cities grow and daily life becomes of necessity more and more mechanized, we inevitably come to have less to do with, even to see less often and to be less aware of, other things which live; and it comes to seem almost as though all the world outside ourselves were inanimate. In so far as the writer thinks of himself as a secretary of society he has that much justification for treating man as a creature whose most significant environment is that of the machines he has built and, to some small extent, the art which he has created. But in so far as the writer is more than a recorder, in so far as he should see deeper than a secretary is required to see, he might be expected to be aware both of the extent to which the fact that man is an animal sharing the earth with other animals is still significantly true, and of the consequences of the extent to which it has actually become less so. Those consequences, though difficult to assess, are certainly enormous and they did not begin to be fully felt until the twentieth century.

The nineteenth century was deeply concerned with what it called "man's place in nature," and as some of the writers pointed out, that had much more than merely scientific implications. It did not imply only, or even most importantly, that man was descended from the apes and was, therefore, still apelike in many of his characteristics. It meant also that animal life supplied the inescapable context of his life, spiritually as well as physically. It meant that life was an adventure which he shared with all living things, that the only clue to himself was in them. But of that fact many, perhaps most, of the most intelligent and cultivated people of our time are unaware. Having to do almost exclusively with other human beings and with machines, they tend to forget what we are and what we are like. Even the graphic arts are forsaking nature so that even on the walls of our apartments the wheel or the lever are more familiar than the flower or the leaf. And perhaps all this is the real reason why we have tended more and more to think about man and society as though they were machines, why we have mechanistic theories about consciousness and about human behavior in general, why we have begun to think that even the brain is something like an electronic calculating machine. After all, it is only with machines that most people are more than casually familiar. And perhaps it is trying to think in this way that makes us unhappy—nearly everybody seems to agree that we are—because we know in our hearts that we are not machines and grow lonesome in a universe where we are little aware of anything else which is not.

In so far then as nature writing has become a special department of literature, consciously concerned with an expression of the individual writer's awareness of something which most people are not aware of; in so far also as it finds readers other than those members of the small group to whom natural history and allied subjects is a hobby like any other unusual interest; then perhaps to that extent what the existence of this department of literature means is simply that it exists principally because works in other departments are no longer concerned with certain truths of fact and feeling which some part of even the general public recognizes as lacking. In any event, at least all of those nature writers who stem ultimately from Thoreau are concerned not only with the aesthetic and hedonistic aspects of the love of nature, but also with what can only be called its moral aspect.

Every now and then the average man looks at a kitten and thinks it is "cute." Or he looks at the stars and they make him feel small. When he thinks either of those things he is being aware of the context of nature, and that is good as far as it goes. But it does not go very far, and there is little in modern life or art to make him go further. What the nature writer is really asking him to do is to explore the meaning of such thoughts and feelings. He is asking him to open his heart and mind to nature as another kind of writer asks him to open them to art or music or literature. Nearly everyone admits that these have something to say that science and sociology cannot say. Nature has something to say that art and literature have not.

But nature writing also implies something more fundamental than that. It also raises the question of the moral consequences of taking that opposite point of view which is now more usual. It raises the question of the effect which forgetting that he is alive may have upon man and his society.

Today the grandest of all disputes is that between those who are determined to manipulate man as though he were a machine and those who hope, on the contrary, to let him grow like an organism. Whether our future is to be totalitarian or free depends entirely upon which side wins the dispute, and the question which side we ourselves are on may in the end depend upon our conception of "man's place in nature." Nearly every taste we cultivate and nearly every choice we make, down to the very decoration of our wall, tends to proclaim where our sympathies lie. Do they suggest a preference for the world which lives and grows or for the world which obeys the laws of the machine? Do they remind us of the natural universe in which every individual thing leads its own individual, unique and rebellious life? Of the universe where nothing, not even one of two leaves, is quite like anything else? Or do they accustom us instead to feel more at home in surroundings where everything suggests only machines and machine parts, which do as they are told and could never have known either joy or desire? In its direct, brutal way even official Marxism recognized that fact when it rested its hopes for a revolution not on the peasants but on the urban proletariat. It is certainly no accident that the totalitarian countries are those which have made mechanistic theories the official philosophy of the state. If man is nothing but a machine, if there are laws of psychology precisely analogous to the laws of physics, then he can be "conditioned" to do and to want whatever his masters decide. Society is then a machine composed of standard parts, and men can be ordered to become whatever cogs and levers the machine happens to require at the moment.

Our forefathers were in no danger of forgetting that they were dependent upon nature and were a part of it. No man who clears forests, grows crops, and tends cattle is. He sees his food coming up out of the ground, and when he would travel further than he can walk, he calls a living, four-footed creature for aid. But unless our civilization should be destroyed as completely as the gloomiest prophets of the atomic age sometimes predict, we shall never again be a rural people and probably we would not want to be. What tools can give us is very much worth having, and the machinery of an industrial society is merely a collection of tools. But our physical as well as our spiritual dependence upon nature is merely obscured, not abolished, and to be unaware of that fact is to be as naïvely obtuse as the child who supposes that cows are no longer necessary because we now get milk from bottles.

In the early stages of mechanized civilization no one thought of mechanics as a threat to the soul of man. The machine was too obviously an alien though useful contrivance. The threat did not arise until we began to be overawed by the lifeless things we had created and to worship, rather than merely to use, our tools. Science and psychology began to talk about the "body machine" and the "brain machine" just about the time when we began to be more and more aware of the artificial rather than the natural environment. When men lived most intimately with things which were alive they thought of themselves as living. When they began, on the contrary, to live most intimately with dead things, they began to suppose that they, too, were dead. And once men were thought of as machines, governments began inevitably to be thought of as merely a method of making the machines operate productively. An engineer does not consider the tastes, the preferences, the desires, or the possible individual talents of the mechanical units he employs. Why should a government concerned with body machines and mechanically conditioned reflexes do so either?

It is highly improbable that we shall ever again lead what a Thoreau would be willing to call a "natural life." Moreover, since not every man has the temperament of a camper, it is not likely that most people will take even periodically to the woods. But there are other ways in which even the urban dweller not fortunate enough to have his country home can remain aware, at least in the important back of his mind, of the fact that his true place is somewhere in nature.

The more complicated life becomes, the more important is the part that symbols play, and all the arts, including the arts of architecture and decoration, are the products of symbolic acts. To plant a garden, a window box, or even to cultivate a house plant is to perform a sort of ritual and thereby to acknowledge, even in the middle of a city, one's awareness that our real kinship is with life, not with mechanism. To hang a picture or to choose a design or a color may be, only a little more remotely, the same thing.

It may be upon such rituals that our fate will ultimately depend. Organisms are rebellious, individual, and self-determining. It is the machine which is manageable and obedient, which always does the expected and behaves as it is told to behave. You can plan for it as you cannot plan for anything which is endowed with a life of its own, because nothing which is alive ever wholly surrenders its liberties. Man will not surrender his unless he forgets that he too belongs among living things.

This is not, in its emphasis at least, quite the same lesson which others at other times have deduced. From nature as from everything else worth studying one gets what at the moment one needs, sometimes perhaps only what at the moment one would like to have. The Wordsworthians, for instance, got the conviction that some pantheistic God who approved of the same thing that they approved of really did exist. Many of us who look back at them are inclined to suspect that what they were contemplating was only a projection of themselves and that Wordsworth might have profited by a little more objective observation—a little more of what he called the scientist's willingness to "botanize upon his mother's grave"—instead of devoting so much of his time to reading into clouds or mountains or sunsets what he liked to find there.

As for myself I settle for what Wordsworth would have considered a good deal less than what he managed to get. What I think I find myself most positively assured of is not that man is divine but only that he is at least not a machine, that he is like an animal, not like even the subtlest electronic contraption. Today in a good many different ways most of us are willing to settle for less than most men at most times got, and that less seems quite enough for me.

In other respects, also, the demands I make upon nature before I will call her sum total "good" are less exorbitant than those which others have made. I do not think that her every prospect pleases or that only man is vile. No one who actually looks at nature rather than at something his fancy reads into her can ever fail to realize that she represents some ultimate things-as-they-are, not some ideal of things-as-he-thinks-they-ought-to-be. There is in her what we call cruelty and also, even more conspicuously, what we call grotesqueness, even what we call comedy. If she warns the so-called realist how limited his conception of reality is, she is no less likely to bring the sentimentalist back, literally, to earth.

How much of the cruelty, the grotesqueness, or the sublimity any given man will see depends no doubt to some considerable extent upon his own temperament, and I suppose it is some indication of mine when I confess that what I see most often and relish the most is, first, the intricate marvel; second, the comedy. To be reminded that one is very much like other members of the animal kingdom is often funny enough, though it is never, like being compared to a machine, merely humiliating. I do not too much mind being somewhat like a cat, a dog, or even a frog, but I resent having it said that even an electronic calculator is like me.

Not very long ago I was pointing out to a friend the courtship of two spiders in a web just outside my door. Most people know that the male is often much smaller than his mate, and nearly everybody knows by now that the female of many species sometimes eats her husband. Both of these things were true of the common kind beside my door, and the insignificant male was quite obviously torn between ardor and caution. He danced forward and then darted back. He approached now from one side and now from the other. He would and he wouldn't.

My friend, no nature student and not much given to observing such creatures, was gratifyingly interested. Presently he could contain himself no longer. "You know," he said thoughtfully, "there is only one difference between that spider and a human male. The spider knows it's dangerous."

That, I maintain, both is and ought to be as much grist for a nature writer's mill as a sunset or a bird song.

When James Russell Lowell reviewed Thoreau's first book, *A Week on the Concord and Merrimack Rivers*, he complained bitterly, "We were bid to a river party —not to be preached at." If any reader who has got as far as this last page feels similarly cheated he may tear out the postscript. Most of the preaching can then go into the wastebasket with it. I would have preferred to have the pages perforated to facilitate the operation, but I am told there would be practical difficulties.